Online Social Support

ONLINE SOCIAL SUPPORT

The Interplay of Social Networks and Computer-Mediated Communication

Antonina Bambina

CAMBRIA
PRESS

YOUNGSTOWN, NEW YORK

Library of Congress Cataloging-in-Publication Data

Bambina, Antonina.
Online social support : the interplay of social networks and computer-mediated communication / Antonina Bambina.
p. cm.
Includes bibliographical references and index.
ISBN 978-1-934043-25-7 (alk. paper)
1. Self-help groups. 2. Computer network resources. 3. Social networks. I. Title.

HV547.B36 2007
361.4—dc22

2007006342

For Andrew and Arthur Buck
and Bonnie Bambina

Table of Contents

LIST OF FIGURES

List of Tables

FOREWORD

The possibilities of computer-mediated communications in shaping human lives and social relations are bounded only by our collective imaginations. We need to go no further than our everyday experiences to witness the transformative power of the internet, or more precisely, the convergence of the triple technological revolutions in computational power, broad bandwidth telecommunications, and digital storage capacity. At minimal or no direct cost to the user, we connect, through our computers, cell phones, and PDA's, to a vast and rapidly growing cyberspace repository of written documents, visual imagery, and auditory expressions. Of equal importance is the profoundly interactive and democratic quality of the current version of the internet. We all have the capabilities to be both contributors to and consumers of this vast cyberspace data repository.

Those of us who work in information-based occupations are well aware of the fundamental ways the internet and its associated technologies have altered how we organize our work day, conduct business, produce and distribute our work-related products.

Social theorists may have failed to anticipate the truly radical impact of the internet on work and economic organization, but at least in hindsight, social theory, albeit with some refinements, makes the unpredicted intelligible. The unprecedented capacity of the internet to compress time and space is the kind of technological breakthrough that is the driving causal force most theories of social change invoked to explain economic transformations and the social imperatives that drive reorganization of work to take maximum advantage of the new efficiencies generated by each wave of technological change

However, social theory has proven much less helpful in explaining the extraordinary extent to which the internet has become a source of sociability and the depth to which it has penetrated the intimate domains of our personal lives. In its most prosaic manifestation, e-mail correspondence has supplanted traditional mail as the medium of choice to keep in touch with our friends, family, and business associates. E-mail's inroads in telephone usage, as our favored means of remote communications, would be even greater were it not for the convergence of computer and telephone as channels of telecommunications. From our computers, we can now IM our friends for real time conversations. By adding a microphone and speaker, our computer becomes a telephone. Through our telephones, we leave text messages and voice mails when real time communications is not possible or desirable. Insert a microchip and our cell phones are able to send and receive e-mails, upload and download information from internet web sites.

The more intriguing theoretical puzzle of the internet is the proliferation of online instrumentalities that allow us to share the intimacies of our life with strangers: chat rooms, blogs, online dating, and the proliferation of all forms of support groups. Antonina Bambina documents in this volume that a search of Yahoo groups yields over 35,000 online support groups. Individuals access these groups to interact with others and share information, emotional support, and companionship

Contrary to these unassailable social trends , pre- internet theories of social support would lead us to conclude that the internet should be an unpromising medium for the proliferation of social support groups. This is not to deny the genuine advantages of the online version of the support group. The internet's anonymity, the convenience to connect at any time and place, and the potential access to large numbers of like-minded individuals offer an attractive option for support and sociability particularly for individuals who because of disability or stigma feel inhibited or even excluded from participation in face-to-face support groups. Despite these virtues, the online support group lacks the very features of the traditional support group—small size, the closed nature of group membership, and the immediacy of direct and recurrent personal contact—that received theory posits foster a trusting group environment that are the necessary conditions for shared intimacies, expressions of felt emotional support and genuine companionship.

Despite these theoretical doubts, Bambina's research and other empirical studies persuasively document that online support groups are capable of conveying not only information and advice, but also emotional support and companionship among strangers with no expectations of direct personal encounters. How is it possible that the internet has become a medium where numerous individuals, all former strangers sharing a common social problem or health condition, find through computer-mediated communications respite from their daily struggles, a genuine source of support and sociability? This is the central theoretical paradox that Bambina investigates in her study of an online cancer support group.

Her research begins with a meticulous qualitative and quantitative content analysis of two weeks of e-mail correspondence exchanged through the SOL-Cancer Forum. She assembles compelling documentation of the multi-dimensional content of social support requested and provided by SOLers. Her research illuminates the surprising range of expressive content in the emails among group members. Another unexpected finding, consistent with other studies of online support groups, is that information and advice about cancer treatment and care occupy a distant third position behind emotional support and expressions of companionship that constitute the preponderant content of e-mail exchanges.

Bambina's most important contribution is to move research beyond the current preoccupation with describing and categorizing the content of online support groups to a more highly detailed exploration of the internal structure of online support groups. She demonstrates that not all individuals logging onto the website benefit equally from the support available from online groups. To create and then appropriate support require that individual members invest time and effort in becoming visible contributors. Bambina elucidates the processes of producing online support through a novel combination of social network analysis to describe the social structure of the support group and organizational contingency theory to predict the types of support requested and provided as a function of social and network positions occupied by support group members.

This book's unique contribution to the current online support literature is Bambina's application of social network analysis. The introduction of social network analysis shifts conceptual imagery of online support from the group to the network as the domain of analysis. In doing so, the network analysis captures the open and ill-defined boundaries of online support from the closed nature of group membership of the traditional face-to-face support group. The network imagery also shifts theoretical attention from the overall texture of email content to the flows of communications among support group members.

Bambina applies social network methodology to explore the internal structuring of the online support group. She measures the volume, direction, and content of message flows between members and constructs network sociograms to display the social patterning of online support. After making a first cut between support givers and takers, she constructs measures of network centrality to distinguish different giver statuses: the star, the singular actor at the center of online activities, and three collective social positions: the prime givers, the serious members and the moderate users.

Bambina applies network analysis to relate how the network statuses patterns who requests and who provides information, emotional support, and companionship. An intriguing side-excursion of her network analysis is an investigation of the extent to which the prime givers may act as a collective functional substitute for the network star. She shows that the prime givers convey ample amounts of support between themselves and with the serious users. However the star plays a unique role in overall network maintenance. The star, in the case of this online support group, is singularly responsible for sustaining contact with the less frequent users and takers in the group.

The second contribution Bambina makes is in applying Eugene Litwak's expanded organizational contingency theory to elucidate the hidden rules and protocols that govern who will request and who will provide different forms of social support. Contingency theory conceives social support as tasks that groups perform, and formulates a series of parallel dimensions for classifying both group structure and task properties (for example group size parallels the number of individuals needed to efficiently perform a task). By identifying optimal matches between group structure and the properties of the tasks they can perform along each dimension, one makes theoretical predictions about relative rates of requests and provisions of different forms of social support. Bambina has adapted Litwak's schema for social support to the unique conditions of online social support. She formulates a multi-level set of group properties that include an individual member's dedication to the group, three properties of dyads, shared intimacy, reciprocity, and the commonality of cancer roles. and finally, the size of group receiving requests for social support. She deduces hypotheses about the affect of each dimension for requesting and providing support that she subjects to empirical testing.

Bambina's research compels us to take a careful look at what is going on in internet communications. She contributes a theoretical framework and a methodology appropriate to the task. As is true for any pioneering work, her methodology will invite more research in the area, leading to further development and refinement. The importance of Bambina's work is that she asks the right questions for a thorough going sociological analysis of computer-mediated social support networks and therefore, points sociological inquiry in the right direction.

Peter Messeri
Associate Professor of Clinical Sociomedical Sciences and
Deputy Chair Doctoral Studies, Sociomedical Sciences,
Mailman School of Public Health Department
of Sociomedical Sciences
Columbia University

Acknowledgments

Peter Messeri has dedicated an immeasurable amount of insight and guidance to this work. His continuing support has made my research possible. I have also benefited from the long-term involvement of David Stark and Eugene Litwak. David Stark infused my ideas with new excitement and dimensions at every meeting. Eugene Litwak generously spent a great amount of time talking through the fundamentals of his theory, which proved invaluable in the conceptualization of my model. Gil Eyal and Rita Kukafka also gave their time to reviewing my work. A number of other colleagues have also contributed to this endeavor, among them Herb Gans, Allan Silver, Theresa Rogers, Cynthia Duarte, Ryan Sperry, and Juliana Blome.

My family and friends have also played a large role in keeping me going. My mother, Bonnie Bambina, has never passed up an opportunity to reiterate her faith in me. Her partner, Jim Went, has been so hospitable during each of my frequent trips back to New York. My brothers' (Francesco and James Bambina) confidence in me always gave me strength. Lastly, my dear friends Karen

Quinlan, Laura O'Kelly, and the other Queens girls wondered why this was taking so long, but still encouraged me to see it through to the end.

Finally, I am grateful to my husband, Andrew Buck, who not only supported me throughout the emotional ups and downs of various stages of this research but, as a fellow sociologist, offered me academic counsel of a caliber that never failed to impress me. There is no doubt that without his support, keen insight, patience, and love this work would not have come to fruition.

ONLINE SOCIAL SUPPORT

CHAPTER 1

INTRODUCTION

The number of people who go online to find support is growing rapidly. Individuals who join an online support group become part of an electronic social network. One benefit of being connected to a social network is the prospect of increased access to valuable resources (Berkman, Glass, Brissette, & Seeman, 2000; Friedmann, 1988; Granovetter, 1973; Wellman & Wortley, 1990). Social support is a primary example of a resource that can be passed through social ties and has demonstrated an ameliorating effect on health and well-being (Kaplan, Cassel, & Gore, 1977; for reviews see Berkman & Breslow 1983; House, Umberson, & Landis, 1988). The electronic social network an online support group creates can potentially provide the benefits of social support traditionally conveyed face-to-face without conventional limitations of material resources, proximity, and temporality. This work examines two weeks of discussion on the SOL-Cancer (Support

OnLine) Forum[1] to clarify the patterns of relations that develop in an online environment and the impact they have on the availability and transmission of social support.

This introductory chapter begins by outlining the most influential social support research and its relevance to this work. The significance and benefit of applying a social network perspective to the analysis of online social support is then presented. This is followed by a discussion detailing the salience of this research for the study of computer-mediated communication and human relations. The research site SOL-Cancer Forum is then described, and the chapter concludes with an explanation of the significance of the work.

The second chapter concentrates on social support found in the discussions on the SOL-Cancer Forum. The presence and kind of support exchanged on the Forum must be documented before the impact of its social structure on the transmission of social support is evaluated. The SOL coding scheme is designed to capture and classify support on the Forum in the form of both requests and provisions. It is assessed by two researchers during the course of three rounds of pilot testing and refinement. The final SOL coding scheme is made up of three larger categories of support containing a total of 11 subcategories that are distinguished according to whether support is requested or provided. The first category of emotional support is made up of the greatest number of subcategories, including understanding/empathy, encouragement, affirmation/validation, sympathy, and caring/concern. Informational support is composed of three subcategories, namely advice, referrals, and teaching. Finally, companionship entails chatting, humor/teasing, and groupness. Support frequencies are tallied for each of these categories and subcategories: They reveal that companionship is the kind of support transmitted on the Forum most often, followed by emotional support and finally informational support.

The chapter ends with a discussion of the significance of these rates in regard to the study of computer-mediated communication (CMC) and social relations.

Once the kinds and extent of support found on the Forum are documented, it is possible to study the network's social structure and its impact on the transmission of support. Social network analysis is used to accomplish these tasks in the third and fourth chapters. The first of these chapters uses a number of network measures to demonstrate the broadly bifurcated nature of the SOL-Cancer Forum's network and its effect on social support. Members of the Forum are found to occupy the position of givers or takers based on their posting activity. The findings demonstrate the pattern of interactions between the two positions is such that the givers impart support to the takers, but the takers do not send any back. However, the kind of support provided to the takers is limited to informational support, whereas the givers supply one another with a wide range of kinds and a varying extent of support.

The second network chapter carries the analysis deeper into the network structure and explores the varied and complex posting activity of the givers. In doing so, four positions or categories of actor emerge from the givers that each occupy a unique role in the network: One category is solely composed of a star actor who provides and receives the greatest amount of support; the second contains six prime givers who provide more support than they receive; third are 10 serious members who exchange a fair amount of support with the other SOLers; and finally 15 moderate users do not receive or provide as much support as the other SOLers, but have a steady presence on the Forum nonetheless. The social structure these positions and roles create affect the transmission of social support such that those who develop the most profound and trusting relationships exchange all kinds of support in great quantities, whereas those less integrated into the network only receive certain kinds of support in lesser amounts. The star actor, the prime givers, and the serious members share a significantly large portion of all three kinds of support. The moderate users receive some emotional support and a greater amount of informational support, but they do not significantly reciprocate either. Finally, the takers do not contribute any support to the Forum and only receive informational support in small quantities.

Thus far the research has documented the kinds of support found on the Forum and the network's social structure. Analyzing the two simultaneously has established the relationship between network relations and the transmission of social support that is present on the Forum. The reasons why the relationship develops in this manner, however, have only been deduced from the analyses and not systematically evaluated. The next two chapters use a theory of optimal matching to demonstrate how and why social support is transmitted within the network's social structure. Expanded organization contingency theory states that the structure of groups varies and the structure of tasks varies such that support will be provided when a group's structure is optimally matched to the structure of a task that will provide support. The task-specific model provides a framework for optimal matching by outlining seven dimensions along which groups and tasks can be matched. The model is modified to be applied to online relations within a social network context by adapting the dimensions to reflect the structure of an electronic social network and online social support. Once designed, the network support-specific model is employed to provide a precise analysis of the interplay between network characteristics and the transmission of social support by matching five structural features of the network with the three categories of social support found on the Forum. To do so, the theory and model are used to generate six hypotheses, one for each category of support requested and provided, that are successively tested. The match between electronic network characteristics and online support is accurately predicted by the model's specifications 85% of the time. Thus the network support-specific model provides an understanding of how social support is transmitting within the SOL-Cancer Forum by describing the kinds of actors who request and provide different supports and explaining why this is the case.

Background of the Study

The influence of social relations on well-being has long been a subject of study across disciplines. In sociology, Emile Durkheim (1951) proposed social relations as the cause of a society's suicide rate. Later, Cobb (1976) and Cassel (1976) introduced the subject to the field of epidemiology with the notion that social support affects health and well-being, and began an era of interdisciplinary social support research. Researchers quickly divided into two camps: those who espoused the buffer effects of social support on stress (Landman-Peeters et al., 2005; Lin, Ensel, Simeone, & Kuo, 1979; Orth-Gomer, 1994; Wallace, 2005) and those who believed that social support had a direct effect on well-being (Berkman & Breslow 1983; Cohen, Teresi, & Holmes, 1987; White & Cant, 2003). Litwak et al. (1989), however, put fourth a unique theory and framework to clarify when social support would be available and how it could impact health (see also Messeri, Silverstein, & Litwak, 1993).

Meanwhile, sociologists who espoused social network theory added yet another dimension to the study of social support by introducing the salience of social network features. Network attributes were shown to facilitate access to some forms of social support and constrain the availability of others. Granovetter (1973), for example, demonstrated how a less dense network with weak ties provided greater access to information about getting a job, whereas Wellman and Gulia (1999) documented that support with large domestic tasks, emergency matters, and long-term assistance was enhanced by a high-density network made up of strong ties.

Traditional social support research focuses on support transmitted through face-to-face interaction in real-world social networks, whereas this work examines social support transmitted through CMC in an electronic social network. It is appropriate that social support research should progress into the realm of online relationships, considering that 70% of American adults used the Internet in 2006 (roughly 141 million) and 58% of adult users accessed an online site for information or support related to a medical or personal situation in 2004 (Pew, 2006). Thus, the purpose of this study is to illuminate and examine social support transmitted through CMC within an electronic social network. Research extending the study of social support into the sphere of online relations must take into consideration the many years of traditional social support research that provide a foundation from which to venture into this newer environment.

TRADITIONAL SOCIAL SUPPORT

The study of social support gained attention with two seminal works by Cassel and Cobb that highlighted the buffering effects of social support. Cassel (1976) put forth the concept that the presence of others acted as a buffer to stress, and Cobb (1976) characterized a sense of belonging, esteem, and being cared for as a buffer during crisis. Two theoretical orientations emerged from these beginnings: the buffer hypothesis and the direct effect hypothesis. The former states that social support provides coping resources that act as a buffer against the psychosocial distress caused by stressful life events (Gore, 1978; Landman-Peeters et al., 2005; Thoits, 1982). The latter hypothesis views social support as creating a sense of being embedded in a social network that generates a feeling of belonging and provides access to a variety of supportive resources (Berkman & Syme, 1979; House, Robbins, & Metzner, 1982; Schoenbach, Kaplan, Fredman, & Kleinbaum, 1986; White & Cant, 2003). However, the strength of either of these axioms has been attenuated by contradictory findings and methodological problems (Berkman, 1985; Kiesler, 1985).

The hypothesis that social support acts as a buffer to stress stems from the finding that although stressful events create psychosocial distress, for some individuals the number of stressful life events does not correspond with the amount of psychosocial distress experienced (Hinkle, 1974; Thoits, 1982). The buffering hypothesis suggests that the presence of adequate social support enhances an individual's ability to cope with stressful events, buffering the amount of psychosocial distress experienced (Jackson, 1992; Pearlin & Aneshensel, 1986; Wallace, 2005). Thus, social support exerts a positive influence on health by diminishing the negative effects of stressful life events (Gore, 1978).

Research has provided support for the buffer hypothesis, however, conceptual and methodological conflicts within this camp have not been adjudicated. Conceptually there is disagreement regarding the notion of coping with stress as either cognitive knowledge of potential resources (Folkman & Lazarus, 1980; House, 1981) or as the activity of coping (Gore, 1985; Pearlin, 1985). Some theorists believe the mere knowledge of social support as a potential resource for coping with a stressful event will attenuate the amount of distress the event causes (French, Rogers, & Cobb, 1974; House, 1981; Lazarus & Launier, 1978). Others feel the level of stress experienced is affected by the activity of coping, that is, "the ways in which people actually respond to stressful situations, [is the result of] the extent and ways in which they draw upon various individuals and social resources that are potentially available" (Gore, 1985, p. 267; for discussion see Sarason, Sarason, Shearin, & Pierce, 1987).

Methodologically the buffer hypothesis is problematic in that stressful life events and social support can be difficult to untangle (Dohrenwend, Dohrenwend, Dodson, & Shrout, 1984; Thoits, 1982; Berkman & Kawachi, 2000). A change in social support, such as divorce, death of a friend, trouble with coworkers, or loss of ties because of geographic mobility can also constitute a stressful life event. Confounding these variables results in a bias in favor of the buffer hypothesis. For example, the finding that greater psychosocial distress is associated with lower social support may actually be because of the death of a spouse, an event that simultaneously increases distress and decreases social support. Measures of social support and stressful life events commonly do not take this potential overlap into consideration.

The direct effect of social support on health is the second vein of research on social support and health. Rather than acting as a buffer to stress, this camp views social support as directly protective of health. Berkman and Breslow (1983) theorize that a "social network provides a web that assures every person in it of receiving a certain amount of emotional and practical support. With strong social support, even someone who is experiencing difficulties does not suffer to the same extent as a more isolated individual" (p. 114). This direct effect has also been characterized as social embeddedness that provides a sense of belonging, reassurance of worth, an opportunity for nurturant behavior, and access to new contacts and diverse information (Berkman, 1984).

Although Berkman and Breslow's (1983) Alameda County Study was one of the most influential early studies of the direct effects of social support on health, in the words of one of its authors, " it was not meant to be an ideal model of how studies in this area ought to proceed. ... [But rather] was meant to be thought provoking and to stimulate research into the area of how human relationships might influence physical health" (Berkman, 1986, p. 560). Nonetheless, most research that followed did not heed this directive. Many studies continued to use rudimentary measures of social support, treating social support and social networks as interchangeable concepts (House et al., 1982; Schoenbach et al., 1986). Even though an individual needs to be tied to others in a social network to have a potential source of social support, social ties do not necessarily provide support or the specific type of support an individual needs. Stokes and Wilson (1984) demonstrate that network size cannot predict the amount of support received (see also Seeman & Berkman, 1988) and Hirsch (1980) reports that mothers returning to college did not get the support they needed from their close-knit family and friends. Clearly, confounding social networks and social support is both theoretically and methodologically inaccurate.

An additional limitation in this area of research is the use of support measures that cannot accurately capture the variability found in the direct effects by gender, race, and age. Marriage has been shown to lead to significant reductions in mortality for men but not women (Berkman & Breslow, 1983), whereas women are found to exchange emotional support more often than men (Liebler & Sandefur, 2002). African Americans are found to rely more heavily on friends and relatives for obtaining social support than on a spouse (Berkman & Breslow 1983), and African American women report more support from family members during pregnancy than do white women (Sagrestano, Feldman, Rini, Woo, & Dunkel-Schetter, 1999). The elderly need more social support for material and emotional needs because their capacities may be diminished (Cohen et al., 1987). Regardless of such findings, the measurement of social support in this area of study does not address these considerations.

To overcome the various limitations of the buffer and direct effect hypotheses some researchers called for a focus on the concept of social support itself. They claimed research in these two areas had proceeded without general agreement as to how social support is defined and without attention to the context in which it was constituted.[2] Indeed, as has been shown, social support had been indiscriminately treated as undefined supportive resources, occurring in a variety of arbitrary interactions and measured as a medley of social integration ranging from marriage alone to scales of numerous relations (Berkman, 1985; Kaplan et al., 1977; Lin, Ye, & Ensel, 1999; for discussion see Hobfoll & Stokes, 1988; House & Kahn, 1985). Under scrutiny, social support was found to be made up of four forms of support that are constituted within two levels of relations.

The four forms that social support can take are emotional aid, information, companionship,[3] and instrumental assistance (Berkman et al., 2000; Knipscheer & Antonucci, 1990; Walker, Wasserman, & Wellman, 1994; Wong, Yoo, & Stewart, 2005; Wortman & Conway, 1985). Emotional or affective support is transmitted through sharing poignant events: congratulations for a well-earned promotion; the expression of empathy with its message that you are not alone; and being surrounded by a group to celebrate life or mourn death. Such expressions provide support by conveying the message that one is cared for and valued (Cobb, 1979; Thoits, 1995; Weiss, 1974). Informational support is the transmission of information and guidance such as advising a friend on a good summer camp for the kids; asking a neighbor the name of her landscaper; or providing a patient with a list of cancer support groups in her area. Knowledge gained from informational support can offer a greater understanding of problems and possible solutions. Additionally, knowing that others have faced a similar problem, and perhaps even overcome it, can provide both relief from personal blame and renewed strength and determination (Schaefer, Coyne, & Lazarus, 1981; Weiss, 1974; Wills, 1985). Companionship is made up of sharing everyday events and ideas such as going shopping, engaging in friendly conversation, and participating in a group together. It provides support by making individuals feel there are people who enjoy their presence and they are a valuable part of something bigger than themselves (Wellman & Wortley, 1990). Lastly, instrumental or practical support includes things like assisting with housecleaning, making a loan for this month's rent, or helping with the grocery shopping. Such assistance provides support by allowing individuals more time and resources to relieve themselves of their daily workloads or the burden of additional assistance needed during a time of crisis (Cobb, 1979; House, 1981; Litwak, 1985). The SOL-Cancer Forum does not contain any face-to-face interaction so support for tasks that require tangible assistance is not possible and instrumental support will not be included in this work.

The two levels of social relation that influence the presence of social support are a social network containing all possible connections for support, and the social ties connecting actors that may transmit support (Berkman et al., 2000; Hall & Wellman, 1985; Parks & Eggert, 1991; Walker et al., 1994). A social network impacts social support in that individuals can only cultivate and access support through relationships contained in their networks. They may not choose to actively pursue all supportive ties available to them, but support that is not contained in relationships within the overall structure of their networks is not even accessible by choice (Pearlin, 1985). On the other hand, small-scale social ties are influential because they are the conduits through which support is transmitted from one individual to another (Wellman & Gulia, 1999).

As has been stated, to overcome the shortcomings in the buffer and direct effect hypotheses, the research discussed thus far focused on the concept of social s upport and the relationships that affect it. Litwak et al. (1989), however, considered the limitations of the two hypotheses to be first-order theoretical constructs. The authors proposed the expanded organizational contingency theory, a second-order theoretical construct that considered the concept of social support and the relations that compose it simultaneously, rather than analyzing the diverse aspects of social support independently. They began by clarifying that the structure of groups varies, for example, primary groups or formal organizations, and the structure of tasks that provide support varies, for example, giving friendly advice or medical advice. Based on this premise, the expanded organizational contingency theory offered a theoretical framework that identified a group as capable of providing support when its structure matched the structure of a task that provided that support.

A task-specific model of detailed optimal matching was developed to apply the expanded organizational contingency theory to the evaluation of the effectiveness of a particular group in providing a specific form of social support (Messeri et al., 1993). The expanded organizational contingency theory offered the theoretical premise that the structure of both groups and tasks could vary; and the task-specific model provided a concrete classification of the two structures according to seven parallel dimensions:[4] proximity, length of commitment, commonality of lifestyle, size, type of motivation, division of labor, and level of technical knowledge. For example, according to the dimension of proximity, a group would be identified as having close continuous contact or distant ad hoc contact, and a task would be identified as benefiting from close continuous contact or distant adhoc contact. Then a group that required close continuous contact could be matched to a task that benefits from close continuous contact thus indicated that group is capable of providing the support entailed in that task. To illustrate, the marital dyad has close continuous contact, whereas kin tend to have more distant ad hoc contact. Nightly meals are prepared mostly in the home on a continuous basis as opposed to celebratory meals that can be held in a distant location on an ad hoc basis. Matching groups and tasks along the dimension of proximity reveals the marital dyad as best suited to providing nightly meals, whereas kin are better suited to providing celebratory meals.

Moreover, when a group can provide a task that is necessary to ameliorate health, there will be a positive relationship between social support and health if that group is present. If the group is not present or there is a mismatch, support will have no influence on health or a negative one.[5] For example, if a cancer patient is suffering from severe fatigue after a chemotherapy session and has no food at home, it would be detrimental to her health if she does not eat or if she has to go food shopping. The task for which the patient needs assistance is not something an oncologist would perform but can be provided by a family member or friend. Hence, having the support of a primary group member may positively influence health, whereas not having a primary group or relying on a doctor for such support could create a negative effect or no effect at all. Conversely, when this patient is in need of chemotherapy to fight her cancer, it will not be a family member or friend who provides such a task but an oncologist.

Accordingly, support from a group will produce a buffer effect when matched with tasks that manage crisis situations, and a main effect when matched with tasks of a preventative nature. Thus, the expanded organization contingency theory exposes both the buffer hypothesis and the direct effect hypothesis as first-order theoretical formulations and overcomes most of the specific limitations of these hypotheses. Stressful life events cannot be confounded with support because life events are not measured, but rather tasks that provide support for life events. Analyzing both the structure of the group and the structure of the task eliminates the possibility of confounding social network measures with measures of social support. Furthermore, the theory provides a framework that can be modified to focus on different groups and/or tasks according to the nature of social support in specific groups such as women, African Americans, or the elderly.

As has been described, the literature on traditional social support describes it as being made up of three kinds of support, composed on two levels of relations. The task-specific model provides a framework for testing a group's ability to provide support and for clarifying the potential benefit of that support. The proposed research will extend the study of social support into the realm of CMC to test the ability of an electronic social network to provide support and determine if the characteristics found in traditional social support are present online. The following discussion delineates the theoretical perspectives that will guide the proposed research.

A Social Network Perspective

Prominent research that has looked at online social support falls into two broad categories: studies of online support groups created for the purpose of research (Barak, 2007; Boberg et al., 1995; Gustafson et al., 2002; Meier, 1997; Weinberg, Schmale, Uken, & Wessel, 1996) and those studies that examine naturally occurring online support groups (Baym, 2000; Brennan, Moore, & Smyth, 1995; McKenna & Bargh, 1998; Rodgers & Chen, 2005; Wright, 2000). In either case, the analysis focuses on the group or individual dyads without considering the larger social network. Those few works that introduce the concept of a social network tend to simply measure the size of the network without conducting any social network analysis or exploring the impact of network connections on the transmission of support (Miyata, 2002; Wright, 2000).

Wellman (1997) succinctly offers a strong rationale for employing a social network perspective for analyzing interactions on the SOL-Cancer Forum by describing how it provides "procedures for detecting structural patterns, seeing how patterns of different types of relationships interrelate, analyzing the implications that structural patterns have for the behavior of network members, and studying the impact on social structures of the characteristics of network members and their social relationships" (p. 179). Social network analysis provides the best tools for this research because it does not aim to clarify how any particular individual uses an online forum but rather the characteristics and patterns of relationships that develop in an online forum, how they interrelate, and their influence on the transmission of social support.

The analytical benefits of applying a social network perspective can be found at a number of levels. Whether focusing on the analysis of a complete network or individual dyads, it is important to keep in mind that every smaller relation, such as a dyad or a triad, is both a unique entity and a component of a successive collection of actors, such as a subgroup or complete network (Wasserman & Galaskiewicz, 1994, p. xiii). Confining analysis to the level of a group that is defined as such a priori or to certain dyads in isolation imposes unnecessary limitations on the explanatory power of social structure. For example, viewing the members of an online forum as a social network rather than a group can enhance the analysis in a number of ways. Making a priori assumptions about the relations between forum members forfeits the ability to distinguish and analyze meaningful group relations from the larger collectivity, which is simply a group in name. As Wellman (1997) argues, "... a bunch of people who hang out together—at work, in a café, or on an Internet discussion group—can be studied as either a group or a social network. Those who study them as groups assume that they know the membership and boundaries of the groups. ... By contrast, those who study such entities as social networks can treat their membership and boundaries as open questions. ... The patterns of relationships become a research question rather than a given" (p. 180). Moreover, the common practice of treating all those who participate in an online forum as a group, that is, a small number of long-term participants who all have relationships with one another, is inaccurate when analyzing naturally occurring[6] Internet forums. They tend to be large in numbers, membership is fluid, and participation varies enormously (Baym, 2000; Mickelson, 1997; Sharf, 1997). Social network analysis reserves the use of the term "group" for meaningful subsets of the larger social networks that have a large extent of connectivity between their members and are tightly knit. Groups can further be specified as a clique where all members have direct relationships or a cluster where a majority, but not all members, have direct relationships. The ability to distinguish and categorize meaningful patterns of relations from the larger collectivity provides the opportunity to analyze their impact on the transmission of social support. For example, Wellman and Gulia (1999) documented that in traditional social networks, support with large domestic tasks, emergency matters, and long-term assistance was enhanced in smaller sized groups with greater connectivity, whereas companionship and information were described as more available in diffuse networks (see also, Haines & Hurlbert, 1992; Walker et al., 1994).

Some researchers have attempted to characterize variations within online groups or forums by categorizing members by level of participation such as heavy, moderate, and light posters (Boberg et al., 1995; Dunham et al., 1998; Korenman & Wyatt, 1996; Rodgers & Chen, 2005). This method does shed some light on the transmission of social support in a forum, however, its focus on the individual limits its ability to offer insight into the relationships formed by different levels of participation. For example, those who are frequent participants are very often posting to each other, creating a distinct clique of members with a greater amount of social support transmitted within that group.

When analyzing individual dyads, a social network perspective takes into account that e-mail exchanged between two members of an online forum does not take place in structural isolation but rather is a tie that is simultaneously embedded within a larger electronic social network and is constitutive of it. Indeed, the provision of social support has been shown to be influenced by the broader level of the entire network as well as the relational level of individual dyads (Parks & Eggert, 1991; Wellman, 1992; Wellman & Frank, 2001). Hall and Wellman (1985) demonstrated that in traditional social networks 46% of East Yorkers' ties stemmed from the larger network structure, thus existing simply because they were located in a larger social structure, and not because of personal attraction or choice. Social ties between two individuals in an online forum are based on their joint membership in the larger electronic network of forum members because participants tend to become acquainted with each other through messages and replies posted to the forum rather than having met previously outside the forum[7] (King & Moreggi, 1998; Rice, 1994; Rodgers & Chen, 2005; Sproull & Kiesler, 1996). An individual can choose whether to engage with another, but it is their joint membership in the forum's larger network that makes their tie possible. Social network analysis allows social ties to be analyzed independently as well as in relation to the larger network that greatly impacts both their existence and usefulness (House et al., 1988; Walker et al., 1994; Wellman, 1981; Wellman & Frank, 2001).

An additional benefit to using a social network perspective to analyze social ties is the ability to have a more nuanced analysis of how social ties operate. Since not all ties provide social support similarly, differences are significant, and uniformity of tie content cannot be assumed. Many replies can be posted to one request in a forum, but it cannot be assumed that every reply contains the same type of support. As Wellman and Wortley (1990) report, "although 87% [of network ties] provide some kind of support..., less than half of the network members (45%) provide both emotional aid and small services" (p. 563). Network analysis provides a means of categorizing ties according to shared characteristics to gain explanatory power over variations in the supportive process of ties. So for example, tie strength categorizes ties according to the level of closeness between two individuals, lending explanatory power to the types of support a tie will transmit. Granovetter (1973) demonstrated how weak ties provided greater access to information about getting a job, whereas Litwak (1985) found that weak ties limited the availability of assistance with activities of daily life.

AN ELECTRONIC SOCIAL NETWORK

Although a social network perspective is best suited for this study, it is not appropriate to treat relations on the Forum as a traditional face-to-face network. The network these actors constitute is more accurately characterized as an electronic social network[8] because all relations on the SOL-Cancer Forum are maintained solely through online interactions. Naturally occurring online forums, like the SOL-Cancer Forum, are not extensions of face-to-face groups, nor are they hybrids of face-to-face groups and online interactions. They are made up of relations that form in a manner and environment like none other. Members make first contact online, and most, if not all, of their interactions stay online so that there is a complete lack of physical interaction or contact.[9] They tend to be large in numbers, prohibiting all participants from having relations with all others, yet, unlike face-to-face social networks, every interaction is broadcast for all members to see. Membership is highly fluid, with low social costs associated with joining or leaving, and participation varies enormously. There are often many lurkers who passively participate by reading posts but never actively form relationships with others (Baym, 2000; Mickelson, 1997; Preece, Nonnecke, & Andrews 2004). At the same time, a core collection of members commonly post messages daily and respond to nearly anyone who posts.

CMC and Social Support

Of the difference cited above, the most significant difference between an electronic social network containing CMC and a traditional social network made up of face-to-face communication is physical. People who are connected electronically need not have physical proximity, and online conversations are carried out without physical cues. Some theorists argue that this creates contacts without intimacy and communication that is impersonal, negative, and uninhibited. Two predominant theories that espouse these propositions are the social presence model and the reduced social cues model (for discussion see Lea & Spears, 1995; Preece & Maloney-Krichmar, 2003). The social presence model posits that the amount of social presence that can be conveyed in a medium determines its ability to foster depth and intimacy in a relationship (Rice, 1993; Short, Williams, & Christie, 1976). The second model, the reduced social cues model, describes how CMC filters out social cues, such as tone of voice, appearance, and physical setting, thereby greatly influencing interactions in ways that tend to be more negative than positive (Sproull & Kiesler, 1991; Walther, Anderson, & Park, 1994). These models led to the conclusion that a lack of intimacy and a tendency toward negative interactions create an environment ill-suited for social interaction or the sharing of emotions (Baron, 1984; Stoll, 1995).

Nonetheless, a simple search for support groups in Yahoo Groups produces over 35,000 online support groups. Individuals access these groups to interact with others and share emotions, information, and companionship. These exchanges take place in electronic social networks through CMC. In their study of a computer-mediated social support network for single young mothers, Dunham et al. (1998) reported "[t]he support messages exchanged in this communication medium were anything but cold, insincere, impersonal, and antisocial events that some have suggested are inevitable in this impoverished medium of communication. Indeed, the majority (56%) of replies expressed positive emotional support and empathy, and were delivered in a context of close personal relationships and a sense of community presumed to be optimal for effective social support" (p. 299). Theorists opposed to the view that physical proximity and cues are essential for intimacy and positive social interaction argue that simply because this has been a traditionally observed norm, it does not indicate that face-to-face interaction is necessary for intimacy and social interaction. Lea and Spears (1995) persuasively argue that "the oral form [has been elevated] over text in modern society; letters and postcards occupied a much stronger role in the development and maintenance of friendships and romantic relationships in the 19th century than they do today" (p. 210). Considering that the empirical work done to support these theories was conducted in a laboratory setting (Baym, 1995; Culnan & Markus, 1987; Parks & Floyd, 1996), it is not surprising that as research moves into a natural setting, findings reflect the wide range of ways CMC is used including emotional expression, social interaction, and humor.

Moreover, studies that have documented social support contained in electronic social networks and transmitted through CMC have not only described online social support as similar to face-to-face support but superior in overcoming certain limitations common to face-to-face support (for review see Chenault, 1998; Robinson & Turner, 2003). For example, in a study of an electronic support group for individuals with eating disorders, Winzelberg (1997) reports that:

> Members of this ESG (electronic support group) used similar helping strategies to those that are found in face-to-face support groups. Members provided emotional support, information, [and] feedback… … Support was provided by members who crossed the traditional boundaries of age, status, and education, thereby supporting the contention that CMC removes the social status communicator. For example, on many occasions teenagers provided support and information to women in their twenties and thirties. Two thirds of the messages were posted between 6 pm and 7 am, indicating that members accessed the ESG during times that they would have been least able to obtain support from healthcare professionals (p. 404).

Accordingly, many theorists contend that electronic social networks and CMC liberate individuals from the confines of physical place, time, and appearance. A physical meeting place has certain hours of operation or a specific meeting time; by contrast, the structure of electronic social networks provides the opportunity to receive support at an actor's own convenience or when s/he most needs it. Someone seeking the support of an experientially similar or dissimilar other can log on to a forum or chat room that caters to that need whenever it arises. The connections made with far-reaching others, such as those in other countries on different time schedules or other night owls, make it possible that someone will be online day or night (Rodgers & Chen, 2005; Weinberg et al., 1996). Moreover, unlike connecting by telephone, an individual can reach out at any time without considering whether the timing is convenient for someone else. The technology also enables an actor to reach many more individuals at one time, even those s/he has no previous relationship with (King & Moreggi, 1998; Rice, 1994; Rodgers & Chen, 2005). Electronic social networks have such extensive ranges that even those in marginal groups will most likely make contact with similar others (Gauthier and Chaudoir 2004; King & Moreggi, 1998; Kling, 1996). Lastly, those who are physically disabled, very ill, or uncomfortable in public can access the highly beneficial support of similar others from home without exerting themselves or burdening someone to transport them (Avery, 1998; Cummings, Sproull, & Kiesler, 2002; Kling, 1996; Sharf, 1997).

SOL-Cancer Forum

The research site for this project is an Internet cancer support forum named SOL-Cancer (Support OnLine) Forum.[10] SOL-Cancer Forum is a virtual space where those who have had cancer touch their lives exchange numerous types of support. It is an unmoderated group active since 1995 that requires only a working e-mail address for membership. The Forum is unmoderated so all messages are posted without prior review by an outside entity (adapted from the SOL-Cancer Forum online disclaimer). Archives of all messages are posted online and publicly available for viewing. The Forum contains men and women of various ages, geographic locations, stages of cancer, and relationships to cancer, for example, patient, caregiver, relative of patient, etc. All the members have had an experience with some kind of cancer; however, how and when they use the Forum for support varies greatly. There are a great number of one-time posters who send a single broadcast message, usually requesting information, and then do not post again. Conversely, there is also a group of faithful members who have posted regularly for years. They refer to themselves as SOLers and consider the SOLers a family.

Data for this research are based on SOL-Cancer's archived discussions containing the contents and logs of all posts and replies. Permission to use the SOL-Cancer Forum discussion archives was given by the owner of the archive and members of the Forum. IRB approval has also been obtained. The sample is made up of discussions that occurred during the first two weeks of March 2000. The owner of the archive granted permission to use any messages posted between the years 1995 and 2000. The year 2000 was chosen because of the proliferation of the Internet in that year compared with the previous years. In addition, choosing the most recent year available increases the likelihood that the sample of individuals interacting on the Forum represents a more diverse population, both demographically and in regard to computer proficiency. The month of March was chosen randomly. In the two-week sample period, 84 members posted a total of 1,149 messages to the Forum. Studies that have analyzed online forums or online support groups have examined records of discussions in intervals ranging from two weeks to one year (Davison, Pennebaker, & Dickerson, 2000; Furlong, 1989; McCormick & McCormick, 1992; Weinberg, Schmale, Uken, & Wessel, 1995; Winzelberg, 1997). A 2-week sample provides ample data for understanding patterns of interactions and the transmission of social support on the Forum given the great volume of messages posted.

Significance of the Study

Having cancer afflict one's life, whether as a patient, a caregiver, a friend, or a family member, can cause a variety of psychosocial distresses as well as great physical discomfort. Patients and caregivers can feel socially isolated and lonely because of limited mobility and the lack of peers who experience and understand the disease in a similar manner. Familial relationships can become strained because of the many emotional, physical, and financial burdens that stem from the disease. Under these conditions it may be difficult for family members to provide each other with support of various kinds or for patients to ask for more support when necessary (Weinberg, Uken, Schmale, & Adamek, 1995; Wright, 2000). An online cancer support forum offers patients, caregivers, and family members access to the kind of social support that can ameliorate such psychosocial distress without the constraints or expenditure required of a physical meeting place and time. Individuals can access this support when they need it, from their homes. Because it is common for cancer patients to experience extreme fatigue, they can also benefit from feeling empowered by the ability to go online when they are feeling strong, regardless of the day or time, without needing the assistance of an already overburdened family member, and accomplish a task independently. All in all, research has documented that online support overcomes barriers of time, place, stigma, fatigue and social isolation (Davison et al., 2000; Dunham et al., 1998; Loader, Muncer, Burrows, Pleace, & Nettleton, 2002; McKenna & Bargh, 1998; Mickelson, 1997; White & Dorman, 2001).

This research makes a significant contribution to the literature on social support in the modern environment of online relations in a number of ways. It lends a sociological perspective to the broader academic community of Internet scholars by adding to the few sociological voices engaged in discussing contemporary issues of online social support and CMC. Approaching the analysis with a social network perspective permits the salience of relationships and the patterns they form in an online environment to be illuminated and clarified. Combining social network analysis and content analysis is a novel approach that extends the inquiry beyond the realm of what users get from online relationships, to understanding the social structure that develops online and how that influences who gets what. In addition, unlike most work on the subject, this study documents how and why social support can be transmitted through CMC in a naturally occurring online group, rather than assuming its presence or the improbability thereof. The network support-specific model provides a tool that identifies the network structures that influence the occurrence of social support on the Forum, thereby providing a clear understanding of when and how each kind of social support will and will not be transmitted. This information can help health care workers, and those experiencing cancer to recognize when an individual should turn to an online support forum for assistance and how to best use a forum to obtain the kind of support needed. The findings from this study show that actors who were most active in the SOL-Cancer Forum had access to all kinds of support because of the types of relationships such participation led to. On the other hand, actors who did not invest in the Forum were generally confined to informational support. Thus, actors who are in need of various forms of support must spend time building the kinds of relationships necessary to acquire the type of support they are searching for. At the same time, those who only want a quick answer and are not able or interested in making a commitment can also get the support they desire. In sum, this study presents in-depth insight into the activity, benefits, and costs of membership in an Internet support forum, contributing a detailed picture of one small part of an environment where millions of people interact daily.

Chapter 2

Online Social Support

A prerequisite to the endeavor of understanding relations in the SOL-Cancer Forum to clarify their impact on the transmission of social support is to establish the kinds and extent of support observed in the Forum. Only after the presence and nature of support is identified is it possible to examine how it is affected by patterns of relations. To that end, a SOL (support online) coding scheme is developed to depict and classify the varied kinds of support exchanged on the Forum. A review of research implementing coding schemes for online social support reveals a lack of consistency in measurement. The SOL coding scheme is a concise coding scheme that extends the study of traditional social support into the realm of online relations and provides a method of distinguishing requests for all kinds of support distinctly from provisions.

The coding scheme is continually evaluated by two researchers and after three rounds of pilot testing and fine tuning, is employed to code all 1,149 messages exchanged during the first two weeks of

March 2000. The final version of the SOL coding scheme contains three larger categories of support made up of a total of 11 subcategories, each of which is differentiated according to whether the support was requested or provided. The frequencies for each category and subcategory are tallied and discussed.

COMPARABILITY OF CODING SCHEMES

A review of coding schemes in the CMC literature reveals that they tend to take one of three general forms: those that stem from traditional social support literature; those that are not influenced by it; and those that are a combination of the two. Each approach is discussed and compared with the SOL coding scheme (Table 2.1), which is then described in the following section.

Coding schemes that are not influenced by social support or other literatures are often developed using a purely inductive method that consists of carrying out a content analysis of all messages or threads included in the data and identifying categories that emerge (Klemm, Hurst, Dearholt, & Trone, 1999; Radin, 2006). Although

Table 2.1. SOL Coding Scheme—Final Version

Support categories	Support subcategories
Emotional support	Understanding/empathy
	Encouragement
	Affirmation/validation
	Sympathy
	Caring/concern
Informational support	Advice
	Referral
	Teaching
Companionship	Chatting
	Humor/teasing
	Groupness

there can be some reward to allowing the data to dictate categories, the benefit of a rich history of research is lost. Moreover, comparing the categories that have emerged from the data in two such studies with those in the SOL coding scheme reveals they capture similar dimensions (Table 2.2). All five categories of support in Radin's coding scheme and the nine in Klemm et al.'s scheme have corresponding categories or subcategories in the SOL coding scheme.

A coding scheme only partial influenced by traditional social support research was developed by Finn (1999) to code helping

Table 2.2. Coding Scheme Comparison—SOL Coding Scheme Compared With Radin's and Klemm et al.'s

SOL coding scheme—relevant categories and subcategories for comparison	Radin message coding scheme—corresponding categories	Klemm et al. message coding scheme—corresponding categories
Emotional support	Support	Personal experience[11]
Informational support	News and information, queries	Information giving/seeking, personal experience
Companionship	Projects	
Encouragement		Encouragement/support
Advice	Activism[12]	Personal opinion, activism
Chatting		Thanks, prayer, miscellaneous
Humor/teasing		Humor
Groupness	Activism	Activism

Radin, P. (2006). To me, it's my life: Medical communication, trust, and activism in cyberspace. Social Science and Medicine, 62, 591–601. Klemm, P., Hurst, M., Dearholt, S., & Trone, S. (1999). Cyber solace: Gender differences on Internet cancer support groups. Computers in Nursing, 17, 65–72.

mechanisms in an online disability self-help group. The scheme was influenced by social support and group work literature and contains a total of 14 categories divided between helping mechanisms that are socioemotional and task oriented in nature. The motivation behind this novel coding scheme appears to be the desire to conform to group work theory, which states that a group needs to satisfy both the socioemotional and the task needs of its members (Finn, 1999). However, an examination of the categories (Table 2.3), once again demonstrates that all but one of them can be found in the SOL coding scheme, which can be divided between socioemotional and task orientated support, if need be.

The only category in Finn's scheme not included in the SOL scheme is damaging statements, which are described as statements

Table 2.3. Coding Scheme Comparison—SOL Coding Scheme Compared With Finn's

SOL coding scheme—relevant subcategories for comparison	Finn helping mechanism coding scheme— corresponding categories
Emotional support	Expressing feelings
Informational support	Asks information, provides information, problem solving
Understanding/empathy	Providing empathy, universality
Chatting	Chit chat, friendship, extra-group relations, taboo topics[13], poetry and art, computer talk
Humor/teasing	Taboo topics
Groupness	Group cohesion

Finn, J. (1999). An exploration of helping processes in an online self-help group focusing on issues of disability. Health and Social Work, 24, 220–231.

that would hurt people's feelings and writing about having your feelings hurt. The latter could be coded as a request for a kind of emotional support or chatting, dependent on whether it was off-topic for the group. The former could be characterized as flaming, which is not included in the SOL coding scheme because it is not a form of social support. This may be a shortcoming of the SOL scheme; however, there have been very few incidents of flaming found in online support groups limiting the usefulness of this category for such sites[14] (VanLear, Sheehan, Withers, & Walker, 2005). Indeed, Finn only logs two incidents of damaging statements over the sampled three-month period, making up less than 1% of all helping mechanisms coded.

Coding schemes that follow the traditional social support literature tend to be one of three kinds: those that employ the three categories of emotional support, information, and companionship (Tichon & Shapiro, 2003); those that use these categories[15] with the addition of esteem support and tangible assistance (Braithwaite, Waldron, & Finn, 1999); and those that replace emotional support with esteem and retain information, companionship, and tangible assistance (Loader et al., 2002). Research employing the second kind of scheme is influenced by the coding scheme developed by Cutrona and Suhr (1992) and work using the latter by Cohen and Wills' (1985) classification of supports that buffer stress. The discrepancies between the coding schemes used in these studies and the SOL scheme lie in the inclusion of tangible assistance and the use of esteem support, either in addition to or in place of emotional support.

Although instrumental (tangible) support is one component of social support discussed in the traditional literature, it is debatable whether it should be measured in research that focuses on relations in online groups that are mostly void of physical contact. Members of the SOL-Cancer Forum are distributed throughout the United States and Canada, and nearly all their interactions take place through the Internet.[16] The small numbers of members who have met face to face have only done so on rare occasions, usually stopping by for a brief visit while vacationing near another member's home. In addition, no messages were found that offer physical assistance, aside from declarations to do something like "come down there and kick your doctor's butt." However, this is more likely a figurative use of language to convey a type of emotional support than an offer to take concrete action. Moreover, instrumental support is often found in very small quantities or not at all in computer-mediated groups (Dunham et al., 1998; Muncer, Burrows, Pleasce, Loader, & Nettleton, 2000; Tichon & Shapiro, 2003). In fact, Braithwaite et al. (1999) coded only 41 instances of tangible assistance, the smallest amount of all kinds of support (2.7%). At the same time, Loader et al. (2002) found only one thread in 149 containing instrumental support. Likewise, there are no instances of it in the SOL-Cancer Forum. Thus instrumental support will not be included in the SOL coding scheme.

Esteem was not found to be a distinct form of social support when statistically tested in traditional social support research. It is subsumed under emotional support in the SOL scheme captured in the subcategory of affirmation/validation defined as acknowledgment and/or positive reinforcement of someone, his or her ideas, attitude, or actions. This subcategory adequately represents esteem support as defined by Braithwaite et al. (1999), as "compliments, validation and relief from blame" (p. 136). Affirmation/validation along with the remaining subcategories of emotional support covers Loader et al.'s (2002) description of esteem support as "both emotional support for people in crisis and posts telling people how good they are" (p. 56).

The SOL Coding Scheme

The SOL coding scheme is theoretically and empirically influenced by a variety of sources. The supracategories of emotional support, informational support, and companionship stem from traditional social support research. The omission of instrumental support and the inclusion of certain subcategories of support are based on substantive knowledge of the SOL-Cancer Forum discussions gleaned by reviewing daily messages for 1 year and a close reading of posts from the first 3 months of the year 2000. The coding scheme used by Braithwaite et al. (1999) provides a good source of inspiration for some of the subcategories of support even though two supracategories of support are not in accord with the SOL scheme. Finally, decisions about subcategories are also based on the iterative testing of the scheme described in the following.

Initially a preliminary coding scheme is developed and subjected to three iterations of pilot testing and fine-tuning to develop the coding scheme that is ultimately employed. A comparison of the first and second columns in Table 2.4 shows the subcategories of support retained from Braithwaite et al.'s scheme.[17] The next few columns detail subcategories that are modified, created, and added, resulting in the final SOL coding scheme presented in the last column. All three informational support subcategories are retained from Braithwaite et al.'s scheme, as well as three emotional support subcategories: understanding/empathy, encouragement, and sympathy. The subcategory of affirmation/validation, which is similar to the category of esteem support in Braithwaite et al.'s scheme, is added during the process of fine-tuning; however, it is subsumed under the category of emotional support. To produce the final version of the SOL scheme, six of Braithwaite et al.'s subcategories are retained, two subcategories from the preliminary version of the SOL scheme are modified, two new subcategories are created, and one is added.

Table 2.4. Designing the SOL Coding Scheme—Subcategories Modified, Created, and Added

Braithwaite et al. coding scheme	Preliminary SOL coding scheme	Subcategories modified	Subcategories created/added	Final SOL coding scheme
		Emotional support		
Relationship				
Physical affection				
Confidentiality				
Sympathy	Sympathy			Sympathy
Understanding or empathy	Understanding/ empathy			Understanding/ empathy
Encouragement	Encouragement	Encouragement		Encouragement
Prayer				
			Caring/concern	Caring/concern
Esteem support				
Validation			Affirmation/ validation	Affirmation/ validation
Compliment				
Relief of blame				
		Informational support		
Advice	Advice			Advice
Referral	Referral			Referral

(continued)

Situation appraisal				
Teaching	Teaching			Teaching
Network support		Companionship		
Access	Chatting			Chatting
Presence	Humor/teasing			Humor/teasing
Companions	Belonging	Belonging		
			Groupness	Groupness

Braithwaite, D., Waldron, V., & Finn, J. (1999). Communication of social support in computer-mediated groups for people with disabilities. Health Communication, 11, 123–151.

EVALUATING THE SOL CODING SCHEME

The preliminary version of the SOL coding scheme was subjected to three rounds of testing and fine-tuning before the final version was complete. The author and a research assistant independently pilot tested each version to evaluate validity. The two coders discussed existing categories and subcategories and then reviewed transcripts of SOL-Cancer while considering the following: the general applicability of the coding scheme; any reoccurring exchange of support not captured by the scheme; and any area of repeated confusion or confounding of subcategories. The researchers then independently coded 50 messages and reconvened to discussion agreement. Each version of the scheme underwent this basic process, with the number of messages coded increasing from 50 to 100 to 400.

Once the final scheme was agreed upon, it was employed by the two researchers to independently code 460 messages, 40% of the entire sample of 1,149 posts. Inter-rater reliability was calculated and simple agreement for all categories and subcategories is above 70%, with the exception of one subcategory, caring/concern, which is 68%.

DESIGNING THE SOL CODING SCHEME

Two subcategories from the preliminary version were modified, and one was created in designing the final scheme. Encouragement, a subcategory of emotional support, was found in two distinct forms during pilot testing necessitating modification. One form is inspiration given to someone in despair who needs uplifting and is consistent with the original definition of attempts to inspire hope and courage, to hearten. The second kind entails commenting on another's ideas or actions as a form of positive reinforcement or compliment. These posts are not about rousing optimism but simply convey agreement or approval. Two separate subcategories were required to accurately reflect and record each unique kind of encouragement. The original subcategory of encouragement remained unchanged, whereas the subcategory of affirmation/validation was created to capture the novel form of emotional support that had emerged. It is defined as positive reinforcement of someone's ideas and/or actions.

Another modification made was a shift in the focus of belonging, a subcategory of companionship. Belonging was defined as reassurance of members and their further participation. It was designed to capture the feeling of belonging to a group discussed in the social psychology (Hirsch, 1980) and social work (Weinberg, Uken, et al., 1995) literatures as an important therapeutic element of support groups. During pilot testing it became evident that the subcategory was not capturing the dimension it was intended to because its description placed the individual at the center of attention, rather than the group. To correct for this, the subcategory was renamed groupness and described as welcoming into the group; requesting permission to participation in the group; and/or speaking of the benefits or actions of the group/website.

After the first pilot test, researchers agreed a new subcategory needed to be created because there was a perennial kind of support that was not being captured by existing subcategories. This support took the form of such interactions as conveying gratitude for sharing experiences, offering distinct statements expressing concern for someone's situation, and relaying information regarding diagnosis and treatment. The following excerpts from SOL-Cancer illustrate these: "Nikki, we appreciate you taking the time out to keep us posted on your Paul."; "I'll be thinking of you while you are at the clinic"; and

> He was dx [diagnosed] 2 yrs ago this August!!!!... Anyway, he had chemo and radiation up till last Dec., then began thalidomide. He is supposed to take it 5xs [times] daily, but refuses and only takes 2.[18]

A number of points became evident after examining many such messages and discussing the underlying dimensions of support they convey. Communicating gratitude and support conveys a kind of emotional support, whereas details regarding diagnosis and treatment are sometimes posted for instrumental purposes and other times for affective reasons. Some posters include such information for the purpose of problem solving because providing specific details increases the likelihood of securing an accurate and useful response. So, for example, someone writes to the group requesting informational support in the form of teaching, "I was wondering if anyone had information on alternative treatments for an adult with acute Leukemia and also congestive heart failure." To ascertain an effective answer to her inquiry, she includes, "He was told that chemotherapy would be too rough on his heart, so he is doing some sort of vitamin therapy at Fox Chase Cancer Center." Consequently, this type of content is not coded as a unique kind of support but merely viewed as part of the request for teaching that it accompanies.

In contrast, other posters discuss diagnosis and treatment to communicate concern and gratitude that is more affective in nature. Initially, a subcategory of emotional support named cancer conversation was created to capture this content. The newly created subcategory proved to be problematic in logging over 150 instances in a pilot test, when the next highest subcategory of emotional support logged only 89. Coders reviewed messages earmarked as cancer conversation and agreed the subcategory was too broad and needed to be refined. A reexamination of this content resulted in it being characterized as taking two forms.

Diagnosis and treatment are often shared with a person experiencing something similar or who had asked about the situation to empathize or to demonstrate caring. Content conveyed to express empathy with another's experience is included in the existing subcategory of understanding/empathy. However, there is no specific emotional support subcategory that captures support given to demonstrate attentiveness and regard for someone's well-being. A subcategory fitting this description was developed and named "caring/concern."

Requesting and Providing Social Support

The final step in designing the coding scheme was to incorporate the ability to distinguish, within every subcategory, whether support was being requested or provided. Transcripts of computer-mediation conversations capture complete support interactions in a natural setting. This offers the opportunity to analyze not only how support is provided but how it is requested. Few researchers studying online social support have attempted to distinguish between requests and provisions of support beyond direct requests for information (Finn, 1999; Radin, 2006). Requesting other kinds of support can be difficult because an individual may feel vulnerable and needy when doing so. Such requests do not often take the form of a direct question and can be hard to identify.

To begin with the two coders recorded whether an instance of support was requested or provided. It quickly became clear that identifying requests for support was not as straightforward as provisions. After the first round of coding, 50 instances of requests were logged compared with 737 provisions. Even though the volume of support provided was expected to be greater than that requested, because support is often provided without being requested in such a group, the counts seemed exceptionally disproportionate.

Informational support was the only category that contained a relatively substantial number of requests, 38, whereas emotional support logged only 10 and companionship a mere 2. Asking for information is commonplace, whereas emotional support or companionship is not something someone generally feels comfortable requesting and often does in a more tacit way. Two facts resulting from this bias were revealed while reexamining messages. First, in the case of companionship coders discovered a number of clear requests for chatting in the form of direct questions that were not previously coded as such. Although these were not tacit, they were overlooked simply because it is out of the ordinary to identify questions exchanged in friendly conversation as requests for companionship. Second, tacit requests for emotional support began to emerge from messages once more attention was given to detecting them. North (1998) explains that when similarly analyzing requests for support in an online group, "...requesting behaviors do take place, but ... are not readily obvious" (p. 40). Therefore, to create a method to systematically code requests, it was necessary to identify and characterize the form they take. To that end, the occurrence of supportive behaviors in the context of everyday face-to-face interactions and traditional support groups was given careful consideration in conjunction with a review of numerous postings and relevant literature (Kim & Bresnahan, 1994; North, 1998; Silver, Wortman, & Crofton, 1985).

This resulted in requests being classified into three commonly occurring styles: clear-cut requests, negative sentiments, and accounts. Clear-cut requests were easily identifiable because they take the form of direct questions where members ask for things like prayers or information. Negative sentiments such as distress, fear, and sorrow convey the need to be assuaged and are more tacit forms of requests. Accounts describing past experiences, prognosis, and updates, whether positive or negative, are also tacit invitations to comment or enter a dialog. An illustration for each of the three kinds of requests is provided below. Each example contains an exchange with a request for support and the subsequent provision of support. All three styles of requests have been found in each category of support.

Clear-cut requests take the form of direct inquiries and, as such, are naturally recognizable. One example of a clear-cut request for informational support is, "My father was recently diagnosed with neuroendocrine cancer. What is the treatment for this? Is this the same thing as poorly differentiated neuroendocrine carcinomas?" Elle responds, providing informational support in the form of referrals, as well as companionship in welcoming the first-time poster to the group. "Hello Friend: Welcome to our forum. Here are some excellent sites to go to that will help you better understand neuroendocrine cancer."

A common form tacit requests take is the expression of negative sentiments such as distress or sorrow. Based on their own experiences, members understand that messages written while in distress are a cry for help even though there is no direct request for assistance. For example, when Murray finds out he and his wife were not informed of a possible negative side effect to one of the many treatments she has received, he expresses great distress:

> I just learned this very dreadful and alarming news. My Libby had 30 treatments of Platinum based chemotherapy in 3 plus years and now we learn that this could lead to secondary cancer... leukemia. Now I learn and wonder why we weren't told at the time she was administered...

The group rallies around Murray with many responses to assuaging his angst. Jenn provides affirmation/validation and understanding in an effort to calm Murray's unspoken fear that he might have made the wrong decision as Libby's caregiver:

> You could not have done otherwise with the information you had then. Any person who has had a cancer diagnosis and chemotherapy has to be watchful but not fearful. You have done very well and we are in awe of your dedication to keeping Libby well.

Another construct used to convey a tacit request for support is posting an account describing one's cancer experience. This can be positive or negative in nature and details a condition update, past experience, or current prognosis. Members share their personal stories to discuss them and the feelings they raise, not simply to have them fall on deaf ears with no response. For instance, when Casey, who is in remission, posts about her checkup, she invites members to share in her happiness, relate to her fear, and soothe her unease about the future:

> Hi, Everyone: I went in for my three month checkup today. Everything is still A okay! I do have to go back in June, though, but after that, it'll only be every six months. Whew! I'm always glad when that's over!

Responses vary in tone and support from simple affirming shouts of "Yippe!!!!!" to Joe's post filled with humor and understanding:

> Dancing the Irish Jig, jumping over barrels, tapping on tables. ... I am so happy for you. ... Believe it or not when you only have to go yearly, you tend to miss your doctor, it's as though something has been taken from you. Seriously!

INSTANCES OF SOCIAL SUPPORT REQUESTED AND PROVIDED

Coders acquired an understanding and familiarity of normalized group behavior and individual style in regard to requests once they were sensitized to them. This knowledge coupled with clear guidelines allowed them to more easily identify subtle forms of requests. Analyzing 40% of messages for inter-rater reliability demonstrated over 75% simple agreement for support requests in every category. Moreover, the proportion of requests coded increased threefold from 6% to 19%[19] of all support. Requests were also more evenly distributed among the three categories (Table 2.5), with information now logging the smallest amount.

Final SOL Coding Scheme

The final SOL coding scheme was now complete (Table 2.1), and all 1,149 messages were coded according to 11 subcategories of support, and as requests or provisions. Thirty-eight percent of messages contained more than one supracategory of support, and nearly all contained more than one subcategory of support. In total, 2,873 instances of support were identified.

The following section presents an overview of the final SOL coding scheme including the definition of each subcategory and an illustration, both in the form of a request and a provision, using excerpts from SOL-Cancer discussions. Each example contains a thread with two posts that demonstrates support

Table 2.5. Descriptive Statistics for Instances of Social Support Requested and Provided—Final SOL Coding Scheme

Support category	Frequency requested	Frequency provided	Percent of total requested	Percent of total provided
Emotional support	163	832	30	35.7
Informational support	115	597	21.2	25.6
Companionship	265	901	48.8	38.7
Total	543	2,330	100	100

Note. N = 2,873 instances of support.

requests and provisions as they naturally occur. A detailed list of the operational measures for each subcategory of the final coding scheme is also provided in Appendix A.

Emotional Support

Emotional support comprises support that is affective and sentimental in nature. The five subcategories are understanding/empathy, encouragement, affirmation/validation, sympathy, and caring/concern. Messages containing emotional support nearly always have multiple subcategories of this support within them and are coded accordingly. For example, a post from Dudley, who is new to the group, contains requests for caring/concern, encouragement, and understanding/empathy:

> … i'm so afraid, this is the hardest day of my life I don't know what I'll do if the news is worse than last itme. Ive been trying to stay positive but the more I read the more afraid I'm getting. does anyone on this list have melanoma and please tell me about your treatment and what they say is going to happen if you can.

Dudley begins with a request for caring/concern described as expressing a need for a great amount of attention and general support. His declaration of building fear, "the more I read the more afraid I'm getting," couches a request for encouragement, defined as expressing despair and/or the need to feel hopeful or courageous. Casey responds with encouragement defined as attempts to inspire hope or courage, to hearten: "I remember so clearly how awful it was, but I'm well today. Hang in there, friend."

Dudley's also requests understanding/empathy. His question, "does anyone on this list have melanoma and please tell me about your treatment and what they say is going to happen if you can," is an appeal for understanding/empathy, described as searching for someone who has an appreciation for or can identify with one's experience or feelings. Casey's response also supplies understanding by appreciating and identifying with his experience by recounting the details of her own cancer story:

> I have to go tomorrow, too—for my two year checkup. I was diagnosed with small cell lung cancer in December of 1997—declared "clean" in March of 1998. I know exactly what you're going through—trust me!

A message posted by Dee contains a request for affirmation/validation in her effort to keep a positive attitude in the face of her mother's failing condition. This is characterized as expressing uncertainty or a need for positive feedback for a difficult course of action, attitude, or decision. Her message also conveys a request for caring/concern with her demonstrating an enhanced need for support:

> ... I don't normally talk to anyone about my Mom because I am sure it makes other people feel bad or weird for me, this is really an ideal place for me to come and vent and listen. God has blessed me Elle, with all of you & that is a great thing to come out of such a terrible ordeal. Someone once said "Out of the worst manure, comes the sweetest roses" SOL has been my sweet rose. It forces me to realize that I am not the only one dealing w/ life & death every day. Not only do other people do it, they do it w/dignity & grace & hope. I hope to emulate the example of The show must go on rather than falling apart. I will not fall apart!!! ...

Members respond with messages demonstrating their care/concern by being very attentive and interested. The numerous posts she receives all provide a variety of support that addresses every one of the many worries expressed in her long message—advice on how to discuss her mom's condition with her young son and to view this time with her mom as a blessing; encouraging pledges of continued support as long as needed; and simple offers of prayer. Elle's message is one such example:

> ... Thank you for the beautiful words, very appreciated... However, the beauty of this world is that we are all different and we all must deal with things the way that suites each the best. ... One of the beauties of a forum like ours is that one can say how they feel and know that it is understood by each and every member. When you try to speak to friends (Outsiders) they are uncomfortable, many are so afraid of cancer and yet so many of us have it, or have a family member who has it. What they don't realize that even though there is much pain, anguish, suffering, there are times of great joy also. To be able to realize what really is important in life is a beautiful lesson. To be given an opportunity of a second chance to straighten up and fly right makes us lucky for the next world. To see the beauty in all people, a glorious lesson. To learn not to hurt a love one, wow, a great lesson. The time you are spending with your mother; the little things you are doing to make her comfortable and happy will always be yours to carry in your heart. Never will you regret it and more importantly after all the years she took care of you, loved you, you are able to give back while she is alive. She wasn't snatched from you at a moment's notice. Now that is joy!

In writing about her "beautiful words" and validating that, as difficult as it may be, taking care of her mother is the best thing Dee could do; Elle's post also provides her with affirmation/validation, defined as compliments, acknowledgement, or positive reinforcement of someone, their ideas, attitudes, or actions.

Sympathy takes the form of a request in Breege's post about her own struggle with cancer in the face of many people in her life who have passed away from it:

> I'd like to borrow the pity pot for awhile if it's free... I lost my best friend to cancer... Her cancer was extremely aggressive and took her from us without even time to say good-bye. Only 2 weeks before I had lost my beloved father... I will try not to sink too low but it would be good to have a "pot" to catch me in case I do...

Her message communicates sorrow and regret for her situation, fulfilling this subcategory's definition. Diane's response contains sympathy, described as expressing sorrow for or feeling troubled by another's situation, "I am so sorry about your losses..."

Informational Support

Informational support is practical in nature and contains three subcategories: advice, referrals, and teaching. Nearly all requests for informational support are direct since it is commonplace to make such requests and does not involve the social cost of vulnerability or require intimacy. A request for advice is described as asking for guidance and is demonstrated in Helen's post inquiring why her doctors cannot adequately explain the reasons for changing her treatment, "I know that cancer is an individual thing and so many different kinds and impossible for even the doctors to keep up with research. How can I help them help me?" Jenn's message provides advice described as guidance, "I would keep asking until you find someone to talk to you until YOU understand the reasons why they want to do this!"

Requests for referrals are defined as inquiries about a source for information or assistance. These are often coupled with requests for another subcategory of informational support, teaching described as asking for instructional or educational informational. A typical request reads, "Can you tell me anything about thalidomide as a cancer treatment? Are there any Web sites I can go to?" The straightforward response includes a number of Web site referrals for information on thalidomide, as well as teaching, defined as providing instructional and/or educational information, which takes the form of factual information about the drug:

> Here are plenty of sites for you to explore regrading the drug thalidomide and its ussages ... The recent data on Thalidomide is very encouraging for some www.healthboards.com/cancer/874.html ... STUDY REPORTED IN THE NOVEMBER 18 ISSUE OF THE NEW ENGLAND JOURNAL OF MEDICINE DEMONSTRATES THAT THALIDOMIDE ACTS AGAINST MULTIPLE MYELOMA http://myeloma.uams.edu/thalidomide.html...

There are some requests for traditional types of referrals such as, "Where do you buy digestive enzymes...?," which also receive direct replies, "I went to a naturopath for this and you buy the enzymes through his office (depends) or at a health food store."

Companionship

Companionship is made up of messages that bestow a sense of being connected to a group and provide support in that individuals feel there are others who enjoy their presence and they are a valuable part of something bigger than themselves (Wellman & Wortley, 1990). The three subcategories are chatting, humor, and belonging. Chatting contains messages about things unrelated to cancer. Requests are often direct questions that prompt social conversations: "Nikki, what part of Michigan (do you live in)?" Messages providing chatting are similarly clear-cut, "I live in Bay Ciy MI (on the bottom of the thumb)."

Humor/teasing general takes one of three forms: writing something that is meant to be humorous; sending a joke; or poking fun at another member. Requests can be direct as in Elle's posts with humorous content about urologists in New York competing "to find the perfect potion, pill or paste to give women perfect orgasms all the time." She asks, "Anyone from Manhattan? I would like to order 1 doz jar's … . ROFLOL[20]!" She receives many humorous responses, such as "I wouldn't touch that one with a ten-foot or any other size pole!"

Coding humor/teasing can require more intricate reasoning with jokes or when teasing someone. All jokes are coded as both a request and provision of support based on the logic that someone tells a joke in a face-to-face setting to provide humor and also to get a response, that is, laughter or a witty comment. Similarly, those "telling" jokes on the Forum would do so not only to provide humor but also to elicit a response. They nearly always receive messages providing humor in the form of "laughter" expressed as "Hah!," "HA!," "LOL," and "Too funny, Jenn!!! …"

Each occurrence of teasing is also coded as both a request and a provision of humor. In a face-to-face setting, an individual teases another not only to be humorous but also to get a rise or response out of that person. This plays out much the same way in the Forum. Elle teases Joe in a group discussion about spending too much time on the "pity pot," that is, feeling sorry for one's self, "Yes, Joe loved the pity pot, almost as though it was a pacifier! One time I had to go to NY and pull the dang thing off. …" Elle's e-mail elicits the expected response from Joe, who teases her in return:

> Now Elle, do I have to tell everyone about the time that you sat on it so long that you got a ring mark! I saw it with my own two eyes when she mooned me… we called it moon over Manhattan ;+) Gotch ya!

Groupness requests are defined as asking permission to or inviting someone to participate in the group. Dudley asks, "What is the protocol on here? Are you all freinds and am I butting in or is this open to anyone?" Another form these requests take is when one member asks another to "Keep us posted" or "Let us know how it turns out." Groupness can be provided by welcoming a newcomer to the group:

> Make yourself at home in this forum Dudley. We are a loose knit virtual family and you've just become our pixel pal! :-))... Welcome to the family!

Provisions are also described as addressing the group or referring to its actions or benefits. One tribute to the virtues of the group reads:

> I want to let you all know that you all feel like family. I've enjoyed reading the banter, the stories, and the fabulous love going over these lines. You're an incredible group.

FREQUENCY OF SOCIAL SUPPORT CATEGORIES AND SUBCATEGORIES

All 1,149 messages were coded using the final SOL coding scheme, and the number of messages containing each category of support was calculated along with the number of messages containing requests and provisions of each (Table 2.6). It is important to note that the total number of messages in the category counts do not equal 1,149 because each message can be coded as more than one kind of support. Similarly, a message can contain both a request and provision of support so the number of messages containing requests and provisions of a category of support does not add up to the total number of messages in that category. Instances of each category and subcategory of support were also tallied, as were the instances of requests and provisions for each (Table 2.7). In this case, the category instances do add up to the total of 2,873, and the subcategory count is equal to the supracategory sum.

Table 2.6. Descriptive Statistics for Messages Containing Social Support Categories—Final SOL Coding Scheme

Support category	Number of messages[a] containing support category	Percent of total messages
Emotional support	554	48.2
Requests	101	
Provisions	519	
Informational support	444	38.6
Requests	90	
Provisions	359	
Companionship	651	56.7
Requests	244	
Provisions	639	

Note. N = 1,149 messages.
[a]*Since many messages contain more than one category of support, category counts do not add up to 1,149, and percentages do not add up to 100. Messages can also contain both a request and provision of support so these do not total the number of messages in any one category.*

Examining support categories reveals that companionship appears in the greatest amount of messages, with the largest number of messages requesting support (Table 2.6) and the greatest number of instances of support, both requested and provided (Table 2.7). In contrast, informational support occurs in the least number of messages, with the smallest number of messages requesting support (Table 2.6) and the fewest instances of support, both requested and provided (Table 2.7). Emotional support falls between the two in every regard.

Shifting the focus to instances of support subcategories (Table 2.7) reveals that chatting records the greatest number of instances (521) and makes up the largest portion of all subcategories of

Table 2.7. Descriptive Statistics for Instances of Social Support Categories and Subcategories—Final SOL Coding Scheme

Support category/ support subcategory	Instances of support requested	Instance of support provided	Total instances of support (percent of total)
Emotional support	163	832	995 (34.6)
Understanding/empathy	35	128	163 (5.7)
Encouragement	54	220	274 (9.5)
Affirmation/validation	28	286	314 (10.9)
Sympathy	9	32	41 (1.4)
Caring/concern	37	166	203 (7.1)
Informational support	115	597	712 (24.8)
Advice	21	122	143 (5)
Referrals	15	210	225 (7.8)
Teaching	79	265	344 (12)
Companionship	265	901	1,166 (40.6)
Chatting	117	404	521 (18.1)
Humor/teasing	117	272	389 (13.5)
Groupness	31	225	256 (8.9)
Total	543	2,330	2,873 (100)

Note. N = 2,873 instances of support.

support (18%). This subcategory constitutes nearly half (45%) of the largest category of companionship. It also tallies the greatest number of instances of the provision of support (404) and matches humor/teasing at 117 with the largest number of requests. Humor/teasing is the second most common form of companionship, and support in general, with 389 occurrences. Groupness is not as large as the two previous subcategories, logging the median number of instances (256) for all subcategories and nearly the median amount for requests for support (31).

Turning to the subcategories of emotional support, affirmation/validation (314) and encouragement (274) are the two largest, with a combined total of 59% of all instances of emotional support. A sample of messages is reviewed to examine the accuracy of this distinction because content originally coded as simply encouragement was divided into these two subcategories. The subcategories held up to scrutiny, indicating that these are two unique forms of emotional support that also happen to be the kinds most often exchanged. Moreover, requests for these subcategories do not mirror this relationship, with encouragement logging the largest number (54) and affirmation/validation nearly the smallest (28). Caring/concern (203) and understanding/empathy (163) tally a fair number of occurrences, and the second (37) and third largest (35) number of requests for this category, respectively. Sympathy has the smallest number of instances (41), not only within emotional support but amongst all types of support and all requests (9).

Teaching is the largest subcategory (344) of informational support, making up roughly half the category (48%). It also contains the third highest number of requests of all subcategories, at 79. Referrals are the next kind most often found, with 225 instances. They do, however, tally the second to last number of requests for support, with a mere 15 instances. Lastly, advice is exchanged least often of all informational support (143) and is the next to last kind of support provided (122) of all subcategories.

These frequencies demonstrate that companionship plays a significant part in members' messages. It is the largest category of support by all measures, indicating that members choose to dedicate a great amount of time to a support that builds and sustains online friendships. Chatting and humor are exchanged often, making up a large part of their interactions, much like face-to-face friendships. Members make initial contact due their experience with cancer, but their interactions lead to more complex relationships that move beyond the disease.

The second most common support, emotional support, is also the most nuanced. Emotional support is composed of five subcategories compared with three for each of the other support categories. Members provide one another with very specific kinds of emotional support to assuage the wide range of emotional needs that stem from the disease. Sympathy logs the smallest amount of all kinds of support, showing that given an array of emotions to choose from, members do not often choose to feel sorry for each other but empathize while providing positive encouragement and affirmations.

Informational support has the smallest presence but still logs a fair number of instances and is included in over 400 messages. In fact, its subcategory of teaching ranks third in all subcategories. This is most likely facilitated by the easy and common practice of cutting and pasting factual information found online into an e-mail. Similarly, a vast majority of referrals are Web pages, although there are some containing traditional sources of assistance, such as the name of a doctor or clinic. The relatively small amount of advice recorded may also stem from the ease with which members can send a URL or cut and paste a blurb compared with composing their own response. Moreover, they may believe this method is more prudent because offering individual advice runs the risk of passing on practices that may be incorrect, ineffective for someone else, or perhaps even harmful. Individuals may attribute more legitimacy to information they find online than to their own advice even though the accuracy of online medical information can not be taken for granted.

CONCLUSION

These findings contribute significantly to the current debate concerning the ability of online relations to transmit social support and the quality of support they may transmit (Baym, 1995; Cummings et al., 2002; Kraut et al., 1998, 2001; Stoll, 1995). This is especially evident when compared with the findings of Tichon and Shapiro (2003), who code online social support with a coding scheme that contains the same three supracategories as the SOL coding scheme. Their research analyzes three months of discussions, 655 messages, on Sibkids, an online support group for children and adolescents whose siblings have special needs. The present work analyzes two weeks of discussions on the SOL-Cancer Forum that contain 1,149 messages. The two groups are both online support groups; however, the purpose, population, and frequency of use differ greatly. Nonetheless, in both groups the kind of support most often exchanged is companionship, followed by emotional support and finally informational support.

The concurrence of these findings sheds light on concerns regarding the ability of online relations to foster high-quality intimate relationships and provide support (Cummings, Butler, & Kraut, 2002; Kraut et al., 1998). Two predominant theories that question the usefulness of online relations for developing intimacy and transmitting support are the social presence model and the reduced social cues model (Lea & Spears, 1995). The social presence model posits that the amount of social presence that can be conveyed in a medium determines its ability to foster depth and intimacy in a relationship (Short et al., 1976). The categories of support found to the greatest extents in both these computer-mediated groups do not substantiate this claim. Informational support that does not require intimate relations would be the only category predictably recorded according to this model. However, this support occurs to the smallest extent in both groups. On the other hand, companionship, which requires the most intimacy, is found in the largest number of messages and registers the largest number of instances of support, 40% of the total. A friendly and profound relationship must be developed for actors to chat about things that go beyond the express purpose of the SOL-Cancer Forum and to bring humor and teasing to this grave experience. In fact, chatting and humor/teasing are the most prevalent subcategories of not only companionship but all forms of support in general.

The reduced social cues model presents another paradigm that views online interactions as socially impaired. This model describes how CMC filters out social cues, such as tone of voice, appearance, and physical setting, thereby greatly influencing interactions in ways that tend to be more negative than positive and creating an environment ill-suited for social interaction or the sharing of emotions (Baron, 1984; Stoll, 1995; for review see Baym, 1995; Sproull & Kiesler, 1991). Once again these assertions are not supported by the findings of these two works. In both cases emotional support was found in a great variety of forms and extent. SOL-Cancer Forum's 80 members send over 500 emotionally supportive messages in a two-week period without the ability to see or hear one another. More than half of these messages containing no less than two out of five different kinds of emotional support.

The SOL coding scheme also extends the study of traditional social support from face-to-face interactions into the realm of online relations. The three supracategories of social support used in the scheme are those most often found in traditional social support research and those identified under statistically scrutiny, with the exception of instrumental aid. Using these three support categories allows a comparison to be made between face-to-face and online social support research to the extent possible.

A novel element of the SOL coding scheme is the addition of a method of distinguishing requests from provisions of all kinds of support. Although some research offers unique categories for coding requests and provisions of informational support, no other scheme does the same for every form of support it contains.

Overall, the social support coded on the SOL-Cancer Forum using the SOL coding scheme demonstrates that the Forum is capable of providing a wide range of support and to a great extent.

CMC can be used to share intimate and sociable messages, as certainly as it can be used to pass on impersonal information. Members can build relationships online that provide the emotional support and companionship they need, or they can simply post a one-time request for information and be similarly satisfied. The SOL-Cancer Forum can supply individuals with the support they seek, providing their engagement with the group is suited to the kind of support they require. The presence of varied kinds of support on the Forum has been established in this chapter, but the nature of the relationships essential to the transmission of each kind of support has only been surmised. The next two chapters will analyze the structure of relations on the Forum to identify the kinds of relationships actors share and how they influence the transmission of social support.

Chapter 3

An Electronic Social Network: A Network Divided

The efficacy of an online forum is not only influenced by its focus and design, but also by the interactions of its members. Different patterns of relations shape the configuration of a group's electronic social network, which in turn affects the transmission of social support among members. The previous chapter provided an orientation to the categories and subcategories of support observed on the SOL-Cancer Forum. This chapter identifies the broad social structure of the online Forum and how it impacts the transmission of the larger categories of social support. The next chapter then delves deeper into the Forum's complexity, providing a more comprehensive description of patterns of interaction and their effect on categories of support. Both chapters impart a general understanding of the SOL-Cancer Forum's social structure and its influence on the exchange of social support.

To clarify the structure of the SOL-Cancer Forum's electronic social network and understand its effect on the transmission of social support, it is necessary to identify salient network positions and uncover the social structure they create. To do so, eight member-by-member matrices are created: two message matrices recording messages sent and received during the first two weeks of March 2000, one of which is binary and the other valued; and six social support matrices representing instances of emotional support, informational support, and companionship sent and received during the same period. Each kind of support has one matrix that is binary and one that is valued. These matrices are then sequentially subjected to a number of network analytic procedures. The first network procedure is the drawing of a sociogram to provide a basic graphic depiction of each network and an intuitive conception of its structure. Observations based on the sociogram are then analyzed using increasingly powerful and complex network procedures including measures of centrality, a core periphery model, and block reduction techniques.

THE MESSAGE MATRICES

The following network procedures were carried out on the two message matrices, each made up of a square member-by-member matrix, one binary and the other valued. Each cell in the binary message matrix records the number of members an actor sent at least one message to during the first two weeks of March 2000. The valued message matrix records the number of messages an actor sent during that period. Unlike the binary matrix, the valued matrix reflects message quantity, not merely the presence or absence of at least one message to each member. Both matrices are directed so that cell *ij* does not contain the same value as cell *ji*. Eighty-four members posted a total of 1,149 messages to the

Forum in this two-week sample period. However, the matrix contains 1,220 connections because any message addressed to more than one member is logged as a message from the sender to each person named. A broadcast message that was posted to the list, but not explicitly or implicitly directed to at least one specific member, is placed on the diagonal of the matrix. It is not possible to represent a broadcast message in the matrix by placing a 1 in each member's cell. First, the data do not contain precise information of the Forum's membership on a daily basis. Although it is known when an actor first posts to the list, the length of time he is a member is unknown. Membership can be assumed for actors who post consistently throughout the sample period. However, for one-time posters, who make up more than half the population, there is no certainty. Thus, it is not possible to discern which actors should receive a 1 as having been sent a broadcast message on any given day without knowledge of the Forum's daily membership. Second, it is not practical to build into the data the assumption that all members who are sent broadcast messages actually read every one. It is far more likely that directed messages are read most often, whereas broadcast messages are treated as optional and greatly influenced by fluctuating constraints on time and attention. This seems especially probable given broadcast messages tend to be either a question from a one-time poster or an informational message containing text from an article relating to cancer and details of where to search for further information.

The Network Sociogram

Initially two sociograms are created from the Forum's valued and binary message matrices using UCINET 6's netdraw function (Borgatti, Everett, & Freeman, 2002) to provide a visual depiction of interactions on the Forum (Figures 3.1 and 3.2). The sociogram in Figure 3.1 is made up of binary ties so that each line signifies the presence of at least one message. The second sociogram in Figure 3.2 represents the valued message matrix, with the thickness of each line demonstrating the volume of messages exchanged between members. In both figures the arrowheads attached to each line indicate the direction messages were sent. Two prominent characteristics of the network are evident: the bifurcated nature of participation; and the star configuration. Members are divided by their tendency to give and take messages or to predominantly just take them, and the volume of messages they exchange. The valued sociogram (Figure 3.2) shows actors clustered close to the center of the graph connected by very thick lines with arrowheads on either side, indicating a large amount of activity in both sending and receiving messages. In contrast, the remaining actors are

Figure 3.1. Sociogram of SOL-Cancer Forum binary message matrix

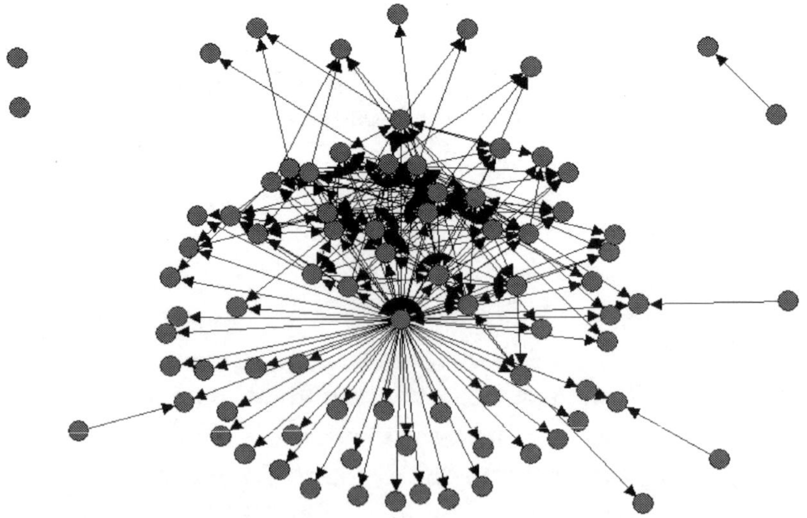

Figure 3.2. Sociogram of SOL-Cancer Forum valued message matrix

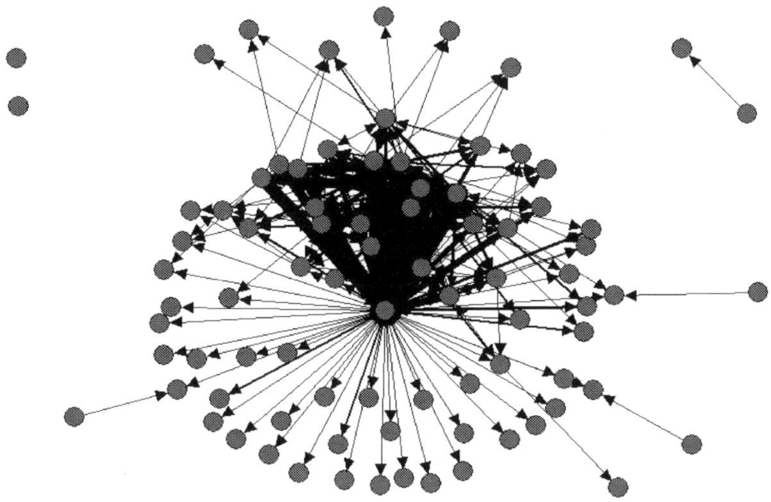

scattered about the network with very thin lines connecting them and arrowheads showing they mostly receive messages without sending any. These observations suggest half the network contains members who exchange a great deal of messages, whereas the other half is actors who simply receive without sending.

The second prominent feature of the network's structure, and perhaps the most obvious, is its star configuration, with a central actor who is connected to nearly all other members of the network. This is an unmoderated forum, and therefore the star formation is not simply the result of a moderator interacting with most actors as dictated by the role. Surrounding the star are two distinct components, a tight-knit cluster of actors and a large number of dispersed and sparsely connected actors. If all actors were directly connected to just one node and had no connections with any others, the network would be dominated by one central actor and the formation would be that of a simple star (Freeman, 1978). However, in this network the star's position of dominance is somewhat attenuated by the tight-knit cluster whose interactions are not limited to the central actor. Almost all these members interact with each other frequently, and some have connections with nodes on the periphery. Notwithstanding, there is clearly a star node who occupies a unique position in the center of the network and is responsible for creating the larger network by uniting the tight-knit cluster with the vast number of members on the periphery who would otherwise be disconnected isolates.

Each of the features observed in the sociograms appears to be a salient structural aspect of the network and, as such, would figure prominently in the transmission of support. However, sociograms are not robust or reliable measures upon which to solely base findings. Sociograms based on the same data set can be configured differently because of the varied methods, at least four in UCINET 6, that can be used to draw them. Thus more powerful and reliable network measures are required to determine whether the sociograms and their interpretations accurately represent the Forum's structure. To that end, the message matrices are subjected to three more network measures conducted at three levels of analysis. In this chapter the bifurcated nature of the network and its effect on the transmission of social support will be the focus of these analyses, and the following chapter will concentrate on the star configuration and the tight-knit cluster that attenuates the star's primacy.

MEASURES OF CENTRALITY

The first two network procedures measure centrality at the network level and the actor level, given the structure of the network depicted in the sociograms. The message matrix must be purged of all isolates to calculate any measure of centrality. It is not possible to compute a valid centrality measure with the inclusion of an actor who is not connected to any other actor in the network because the node is infinitely distant from all other nodes (Wasserman & Faust, 1994, p. 187). Thus, the four actors meeting this requirement are removed from the matrix, leaving a connected network of 80 members.

Because of the public nature of all interactions on the Forum, a Freeman Degree measure of centrality is chosen over measures of closeness or betweenness because it is an "activity based," straightforward count of the number of direct interactions each actor has with every other actor (Freeman, 1978). Closeness, on the other hand, is a measure of how close or distant an actor is to all others. It is used to determine the level of access each actor has to other members (Wasserman & Faust, 1994). An actor's closeness measure is useful for identifying his or her communicative position and level of independence in relying on others to pass on messages. Betweenness is a measure of an actor's position between two other members along the shortest path, or geodesic, that connects them, indicating a potential position of power (Wasserman & Faust, 1994). This measure illustrates the amount of control and influence an actor can have over the interactions and the flow of information between those connected through him (Degenne & Forsé, 1999; Scott, 1991). However, in an online forum all messages are posted to all members and can be responded to by anyone creating a network where these forms of communication dependence and control are not present. Given the public and open lines of communication in an online forum, measuring centrality with Freeman Degrees is most meaningful and appropriate.

A Network Divided

The sociograms displayed in Figures 3.1 and 3.2 present a network that appears to be divided between actors who are very active in both giving and receiving, and those who participate very little, mostly receiving messages. To verify this observation, first network centralization is calculated to determine the extent of centralization in message sending and receiving at the system level. Next, the degree of centrality for each actor is computed, offering a detailed analysis of exchange patterns in the network at the actor level. Lastly, a blockmodel provides an analysis of aggregate level positions and how they relate to one another.

Network Centralization

At the network level, centralization is a measure of the "sum of the differences between the maximal centrality of one point and the centrality of every other point" (Degenne & Forsé 1999, p. 134). The network centralization index for the SOL-Cancer Forum is calculated on the binary member-by-member matrix purged of all isolates using UCINET 6. Centrality is measured in both outdegree and indegree because the relations in this network are directed. The outdegree centralization index indicates the degree to which actors in the network are chosen by, or receive messages from, a central actor(s), that is, how cohesive the network is around a center in regard to messages being sent out from it. The lower the index, the larger the number of nodes who share a similar position in sending messages, as opposed to a central node(s) sending messages to proportionately more actors. Conversely, the indegree centralization index demonstrates the degree to which the actors in the network choose, or send messages to, a central actor(s), that is, how cohesive the network is around a center in regard to messages coming into it. The lower the indegree centralization index, the larger the number of nodes who share a similar position in receiving messages, as opposed to a central node(s) receiving messages from proportionately more actors (Scott, 1991).

The SOL-Cancer network's outdegree centralization index, expressed as a percentage, is 83% and the indegree centralization index is 24%. The great variation between these two measures supports the notion of a disparity in members' practices of sending and receiving messages. The outdegree centralization of 83% indicates that message sending is highly concentrated in the network. An index equaled to 1, or as a percentage 100%, would mean that one node dominated all others in occupying the central role in sending messages. However, a high index that does not reach 1 suggests this network contains a group of centralized actors who send out a great proportion of messages. In contrast, the indegree centralization of 24% is not highly concentrated and characterizes the network as one in which actors who receive messages tend to be dispersed rather then centrally located in the graph. A large percentage would point to a highly concentrated small number of actors receiving messages, so this small percentage further indicates that most nodes in the network receive messages.

These centralization indexes establish the bifurcated nature of the network made up of givers and takers. The givers make up the smaller highly concentrated group whose message sending activity is reflected in the high outdegree index. These members send messages to a much larger disperse group of receivers who do not reciprocate, resulting in the small indegree centralization index. The following analysis of actor level centrality provides further confirmation of this finding at a more detailed level.

Actor Centrality

At the individual level, centrality measures the distance between any particular actor and all other actors. Freeman Degrees are calculated for all the actors using the binary matrix and the valued matrix. Measures of outdegree and indegree are necessary, given the asymmetric nature of the matrices. The binary outdegree represents the number of members to whom an actor sends messages, and the valued outdegree is the total number of messages an actor has sent. The binary indegree, on the other hand, signifies the number of members from whom an actor receives messages, and the valued indegree the total number of messages an actor has received. The findings are presented in two tables such that those actors who sent a message to at least one member are included in Table 3.1 and those who did not send any directed message are in Table 3.2.

The first column of each table presents actors' binary outdegrees, or the number of individuals at least one message was sent to. The next column displays actors' binary indegrees, or the number of people who have sent at least one message to them. The third column includes the difference between these two measures, so that the disparity between the number of members an actor sent to and received from can be assessed. The second half of both tables contains the valued degrees for each actor, indicating the number of messages each actor sent (valued outdegree) and received (valued indegree). The final column demonstrates the difference between the number of messages each actor sent and received.

The findings presented in these tables substantiate the highly concentrated outdegree centralization index and the more dispersed indegree centralization index. Over half (48) of the 80 network members have a binary outdegree of zero, whereas only 3 members have a binary indegree of zero. Thus, although more than half the network did not provide a message to any other member, all members, except 3, received one from at least one other member. As such, 48 members of the SOL-Cancer Forum constitute the takers with outdegrees uniformly at zero and indegrees ranging from 1 to 4. In network terms, these members are labeled "receivers" because they only have indegree counts and no outdegrees (Marsden, 1989; Wasserman & Faust, 1994). Conversely,

Table 3.1. Freeman Degree Centrality Measures—Binary and Valued Relations of Message Matrices—"Givers"

	Binary Freeman Degrees			Valued Freeman Degrees		
	Outdegree	Indegree	Difference	Outdegree	Indegree	Difference
Elle	69	23	46	200	187	13
Casey	28	20	8	127	80	47
Dee	24	15	9	64	49	15
Murray	21	17	4	77	59	18
Jenn	19	16	3	59	42	17
Nikki	15	12	3	50	35	15
Robin	15	16	–1	44	48	–4
Breege	15	12	3	29	27	2
GwenQ	11	12	–1	29	33	–4
Helen	11	5	6	24	18	6
Tessy	11	8	3	18	12	6
Chad	11	13	–2	15	20	–5
Stella	10	8	2	23	25	–2
Joe	9	7	2	30	29	1
May	9	10	–1	17	24	–7
NikkiJ	8	8	0	20	20	0
Dudley	8	9	–1	15	19	–4
Diane	8	9	–1	8	16	–8
Kelly	6	5	1	10	11	–1

(continued)

Table 3.1. *(continued)* Freeman Degree Centrality Measures—Binary and Valued Relations of Message Matrices—"Givers"

	Binary Freeman Degrees			Valued Freeman Degrees		
	Outdegree	Indegree	Difference	Outdegree	Indegree	Difference
MargoH	6	7	–1	9	11	–2
Marianne	6	5	1	7	7	0
Jessica	5	5	0	8	10	–2
FrankieO	3	4	–1	7	10	–3
MaryS	3	5	–2	4	8	–4
Denise	3	4	–1	3	5	–2
Lucia	3	6	–3	3	11	–8
Jane	2	2	0	5	4	1
Sophia	1	4	–3	1	5	–4
Cracker	1	0	1	1	0	1
No1Fan	1	0	1	1	0	1
Anthony	1	3	–2	1	3	–2
Amber	1	0	1	1	0	1

Table 3.2. Freeman Degree Centrality Measures—Binary and Valued Relations of Message Matrices—"Takers"

	Binary Freeman Degrees			Valued Freeman Degrees		
	Outdegree	Indegree	Difference	Outdegree	Indegree	Difference
Ron	0	4	–4	0	5	–5
Jennifer	0	4	–4	0	5	–5
Joan	0	3	–3	0	3	–3
JuneR	0	3	–3	0	3	–3
Maureen	0	3	–3	0	3	–3
StacyN	0	3	–3	0	3	–3
Keming	0	3	–3	0	3	–3
Karen	0	2	–2	0	4	–4
Lorella	0	2	–2	0	3	–3
CMD	0	2	–2	0	3	–3
Bob	0	2	–2	0	2	–2
MikeK	0	2	–2	0	2	–2
Ann	0	2	–2	0	2	–2
O'Kelly	0	2	–2	0	2	–2
Pen	0	2	–2	0	2	–2
Ethel	0	2	–2	0	2	–2
Jamie	0	2	–2	0	2	–2
Stacey	0	1	–1	0	2	–2
Tony	0	1	–1	0	2	–2

(continued)

Table 3.2. *(continued)* Freeman Degree Centrality Measures—Binary and Valued Relations of Message Matrices—"Takers"

	Binary Freeman Degrees			Valued Freeman Degrees		
	Outdegree	Indegree	Difference	Outdegree	Indegree	Difference
Rhea	0	1	–1	0	1	–1
CIGPIC	0	1	–1	0	1	–1
RRB	0	1	–1	0	1	–1
RLBrobook	0	1	–1	0	1	–1
Rob	0	1	–1	0	1	–1
Tami	0	1	–1	0	1	–1
Christina	0	1	–1	0	1	–1
Jan	0	1	–1	0	1	–1
DavidB	0	1	–1	0	1	–1
Larry	0	1	–1	0	1	–1
Helga	0	1	–1	0	1	–1
Edith	0	1	–1	0	1	–1
Dkny	0	1	–1	0	1	–1
Ray	0	1	–1	0	1	–1
Jeffrey	0	1	–1	0	1	–1
Cathy	0	1	–1	0	1	–1
Jose	0	1	–1	0	1	–1
Emily	0	1	–1	0	1	–1
MGMLMC	0	1	–1	0	1	–1

(continued)

Table 3.2. *(continued)* Freeman Degree Centrality Measures—Binary and Valued Relations of Message Matrices—"Takers"

	Binary Freeman Degrees			Valued Freeman Degrees		
	Outdegree	Indegree	Difference	Outdegree	Indegree	Difference
MrsFarm	0	1	–1	0	1	–1
MrsSperi	0	1	–1	0	1	–1
Violet	0	1	–1	0	1	–1
Florence	0	1	–1	0	1	–1
Candy	0	1	–1	0	1	–1
Josephine	0	1	–1	0	1	–1
chatnj	0	1	–1	0	1	–1
JAT	0	1	–1	0	1	–1
Conman	0	1	–1	0	1	–1
Vitali	0	1	–1	0	1	–1

the remaining 32 members are the givers, sending messages to a median number of 8 actors and a mean of 9.[21] These actors are characterized as "givers" even though they also receive messages because in comparison to the takers, who send no directed messages, they are responsible for all the giving. They also tend to give more messages than they receive, with 59% of them sending messages to more members than they acquire from.

An examination of actors' valued degrees highlights the extent of the discrepancy between the takers and the givers when the numbers of messages sent and received are considered. Whereas there is no change in outdegree for the takers, 75% of the givers show an increase in outdegree, indicating that more than one message was sent to at least one other member. The posting activity of these actors has an enormous range, extending from just one message sent to 200 messages sent. Measures of central tendency provide a better description of the givers' posting activity as a whole, considering these extremes. The median number of messages sent is 15 and the mean 28.

The entire range of Freeman Degrees presented supports the notion of a bifurcated network. Thus far, findings at both the network level and the actor level establish the network as one divided by patterns of giving and taking support messages. In the following section, members of the SOL-Cancer Forum are grouped into these two positions, and the relationship between them is examined to demonstrate that the finding holds at the aggregate level as well.

Blockmodeling

Blockmodeling is a method used to simplify complex network relations and provide a clear picture of a network's social structure. To create a blockmodel, actors are aggregated into positions according to shared patterns of ties in the network, and the relations between positions are then identified. In this way a complete blockmodel is constructed and the network's social structure is revealed.

To construct a blockmodel to describe the social structure of the SOL-Cancer Forum, the binary message matrix was subjected to the CONCOR function of UCINET 6, which "partitions the population in a way that may be intuitively characterized as yielding sharp contrasts in densities of ties between different blocks" (White, Boorman, & Breiger, 1976, p. 745). Specifically, this function iteratively creates correlation matrices until there is a convergence of correlations such that each cell contains a 1 or –1. The data are then split into two blocks with those members who are positively correlated in one block and those with whom they are negatively correlated in the other (Borgatti et al., 2002). The densities of ties between and within blocks are calculated once actors are partitioned into blocks. A density cutoff point is decided upon that is used to designate each block as either a oneblock, indicating substantially dense relations, or a zeroblock, made up of sparse relations. The average density of all the blocks is commonly used as the cutoff density; however, this can vary, based on substantive justification.

CONCOR was run on the binary message matrix without including the transpose to allow a direct comparison and assessment of the division in the network based on the actor level Freeman outdegrees presented in the foregoing. The actors in each of the two blocks resulting from CONCOR's partition are nearly exactly identical to the division created by the Freeman outdegrees. The exceptions are three actors who send only one message each and are now grouped with the takers rather than the givers. The density of ties within and between the two blocks presented in Table 3.3 demonstrates that actors in the first block send a great number of messages to one another and a few to those in the second block, whereas actors in the second block do not send messages to anyone. These densities further justify a network divided between those who give support messages, both to themselves and others, and those who receive them without giving.

Table 3.3. Density Table for SOL-Cancer Forum—Binary Data

	1	2
1	0.333	0.048
2	0.000	0.001

Figure 3.3. Blockmodel image for SOL-Cancer Forum—average density cutoff

1	**0**
0	**0**

The average density of the matrix (.095) suggested by CONCOR as the zeroblock threshold is applied to the density of each cell to convert the density table into a blockmodel image. This cutoff point results in a blockmodel representing a social structure slightly different from the one presented thus far. White et al. (1976) interpret the pattern displayed in Figure 3.3 as a network containing one clique and the remaining isolates. This does not suggest a structure composed of givers and takers. However, its emergence is not difficult to explain considering that 65% of the members in the second block receive a message from only one actor in the first block. As such, the connection from the first block to the second is not highly dense (.048) even though there are ties there. In some networks this may justify considering the members in the second block as isolates, but a reading of the messages exchanged on the SOL-Cancer Forum makes it clear that these members are as connected as they want to be. The one message they receive contains an answer to their question and a statement welcoming them to the group. It is of their choosing not to continue the dialog and have more ties with the Forum. A few newcomers did choose to respond and established numerous ties with other members to the extent that these actors were grouped with the first block. Another factor contributing to the pattern of this blockmodel is the very great number of members in the first block who have a connection with one another. This results in the high density of ties within the first block and an increase in the average density of the entire matrix.

One acceptable practice in refining a blockmodel to more accurately represent substantive network relations is to reduce the cutoff point to half the average density. The average density is commonly used as a cutoff point, but it is not the only cutoff that is accepted or employed. In fact Wasserman and Faust (1994) report that "[r]esearch has shown that global interpretations of blockmodels are quite robust under reasonable changes in values of α [the density criterion] used to define oneblocks" (p. 401). Moreover, White et al. (1976) clearly state that "[t]he image suggested by CONCOR can be refined by varying the cutoff level of tie density below which a block is coded as a zeroblock" (p. 745). The authors then go on to reduce an average density cutoff point by half to refine the interpretation of a blockmodel based on a substantive understanding of the data. In the case of the SOL-Cancer blockmodel, the density of ties from Block 1 to Block 2 is much greater than the nearly nonexistent ties from or within the second block even if it is not above the average cutoff point. The presence of ties from Block 1 to Block 2 is much more significant in light of the absence of any in the remaining two cells. Salient information about ties in the Forum will be lost if all three of these cells are similarly categorized as zeroblocks. This is confirmed by previous findings presented in the foregoing, and the content of messages containing substantive evidence of network relations. Refining the blockmodel above by reducing the cutoff point by one half (.0475) results in the image presented in Figure 3.4. Turning once again to White et al.'s (1976) description of basic blockmodels, this blockmodel represents a network of actors divided between active members who give to themselves and others, and passive members who do not give to anyone. Furthermore, focusing on the diagonal cells of the blockmodel suggests that the givers possess a group identity whereas the takers do not. A oneblock in the givers' self-referential cell demonstrates that they have very dense ties with one another and interact as a group. The takers have a self-referential zeroblock, implying they do not interact with one another at all. Overall, the results from the density table and refined blockmodel image are in keeping with network and actor level findings demonstrating that the SOL-Cancer Forum has a bifurcated network, with the givers sending support messages to themselves and to the takers, and the takers not sending to each other or to the givers.

Figure 3.4. Blockmodel image for SOL-Cancer Forum—binary data—one half average density cutoff

1	1
0	0

A positional analysis of the valued matrix, which contains not just the number of actors contacted but the total volume of messages sent, once again provides an enhanced picture of the discrepancy between the givers and the takers. There is no change in actor grouping from that found in the binary matrix when CONCOR is conducted on the valued matrix, yet there is a great increase in the discrepancy between the densities of messages sent by each group. A comparison between the density tables for the SOL-Cancer Forum using the binary data (Table 3.3) and the valued data (Table 3.4) clearly shows that the large disparity stems from a lack of change in the takers' activity compared with a great rise in the density of ties among the givers.

Table 3.4. Density Table for SOL-Cancer Forum Blockmodel—Valued Data

	1	2
1	1.020	0.053
2	0.000	0.001

Figure 3.5. Blockmodel image for SOL-Cancer Forum—valued data

1	**0**
0	**0**

The blockmodel image (Figure 3.5) created from the density table of the valued data shows that when the quantity of ties is considered the social structure of the Forum definitely takes on the form of a network with one clique and the remaining isolates. The valued data blockmodel retains this social structure whether the average density of .269 is used as a cutoff point or half the density, .135, unlike the blockmodel based on the binary data representing the number of members contacted. Thus, the valued findings, both alone and when compared with the binary results, suggest that moving beyond the number of actors contacted reveals a more intricate contrast between the two halves of the network than simply giving or taking. The takers display a pattern of static and rudimentary involvement with the Forum that remains unchanged when the number of messages sent is considered. On the other hand, the density of ties among the givers doubles because of the highly dynamic and elaborate participation of these members. This comparison also reveals that even though the givers have a complex relationship with one another, their relationship to the takers is as one-dimensional as the takers themselves, exhibiting barely any change (.005) when the number of messages sent is included. Thus, the givers do make up a dense clique and the takers are relatively isolated when measuring the strength of contact rather than its presence or absence.

Overall, the findings thus far converge on a network that is broadly made up of two categories of actors: a group of active members who both send and receive support messages and a group of highly inactive members who predominantly only receive support messages. The contact made among members of the network depicted in the sociograms, measures of network centralization, actor-level binary Freeman Degrees, and the binary positional analysis all demonstrate that the givers are densely connected to one another and make some contact with the takers, whereas the takers initiate very little contact with anyone. Delving deeper into the network's dynamics by analyzing the quantity of contact among network members, using both valued Freeman Degrees and a positional analysis of valued data, reveals the profound gulf between the scope and vigor of the givers and the uniformly stagnant participation of the takers. This finding mirrors the activity of these two groups, visually depicted in the valued sociogram (Figure 3.1) that began the investigation.

THE TRANSMISSION OF SOCIAL SUPPORT

The effects of the network's configuration and the social structure of message sending on the transmission of support can now be determined by examining the content of messages. The following support matrices are created using the counts of instances of support in messages sent from one actor to another. The contents of all 1,149 messages sent during the sample period were coded for emotional support, informational support, and companionship, and two member-by-member matrices, one binary and one valued, for each type of support are created based on coding counts. Initially these matrices are used to generate one composite sociogram representing all the social support exchanged within the network. The two matrices of each type of support are then successively mapped onto this basic configuration so that a clear depiction of the variation in support networks can be displayed. The matrices are further subjected to more powerful network measures, such as centrality and blockmodeling, analogous to those applied to the message network in the foregoing. The division between the givers and the takers initially presented in Tables 3.1 and 3.2 is maintained throughout the analyses assessing the influence of the bifurcated network structure on the transmission of support. This allows a comparison with earlier findings but prohibits a measure of network-level centralization of the support networks because it can only be calculated when all isolates are removed from the network. It is not possible to remove each network's isolates and maintain comparability among them, given the variation in participation between the message network and each of three support networks. Nonetheless, actor-level centrality measures and aggregate-level blockmodeling techniques are not similarly affected by isolates and will provide ample insight into the support networks. In addition, sociograms do present illustrations of supportive interactions at the network level even if they are somewhat basic and not very robust. The division between the givers and the takers is not imposed when creating the support sociograms and the unadulterated support matrices are used.

The Composite Social Support Sociogram

The sociogram in Figure 3.6 is constructed from the three binary support matrices and displays all connections containing social support in the SOL-Cancer Forum. Considering that a network of all three kinds of support would contain nearly every connection made on the Forum, it is not surprising that the overall configuration of the composite support network is very similar to that of

Figure 3.6. Sociogram of composite social support matrices—binary

the message network; that is, it appears to be divided between a close-knit cluster of actors and a collection of disperse actors with one central actor uniting them. However, when each support network is examined individually, the difference in the kinds of support exchanged within and between the two halves of the network emerges. Each support network will be mapped onto this basic configuration of the composite support network to lend clarity to the distinction between the three networks. This is followed by an examination of actor-level Freeman Degrees and aggregate-level positional analysis for each type of support.

Emotional Support

The sociograms in Figures 3.7 and 3.8 are created using the two member-by-member emotional support matrices. The binary

Figure 3.7. Sociogram of binary emotional support matrix

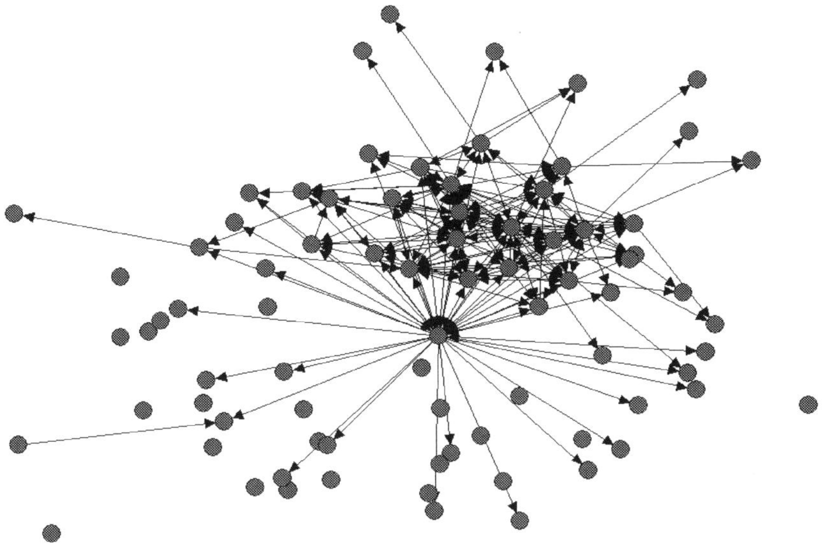

Figure 3.8. Sociogram of valued emotional support matrix

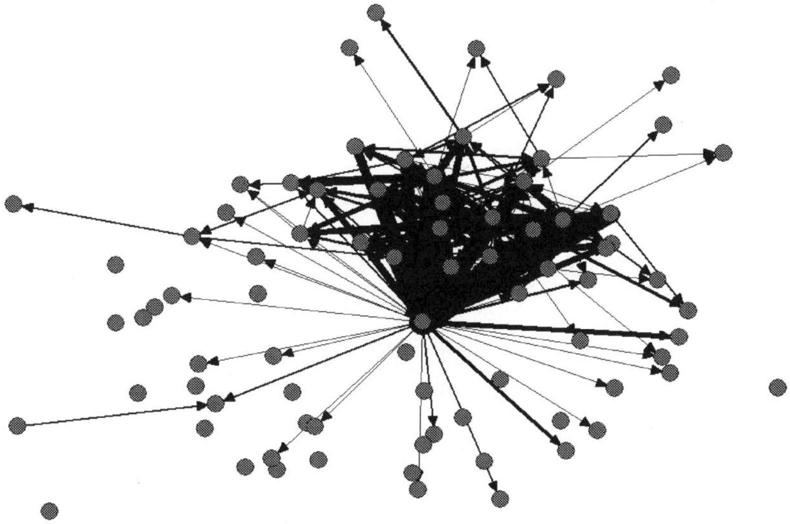

matrix that logs the presence of at least one instance of emotional support is presented in Figure 3.7, and the valued matrix that logs all instances of emotional support is presented in Figure 3.8. The binary sociogram demonstrates that the emotional support network maintains an overall pattern similar to the message network in that the exchange of emotional support is more highly concentrated among a tight-knit cluster of actors. However, unlike the message network's sociogram, there are far fewer actors included in the emotional support network.

The extent of this discrepancy is enhanced in the valued sociogram (Figure 3.8) reflecting not only the members included in the network but also the volume of messages, represented by the thickness of each line. In both sociograms the notion of support takers appears to be supported by the one-sided arrowheads on most lines connecting the sparse actors to the network. There are too many interactions within the tight-knit cluster to accurately assess the direction of all connections visually, but considering the abundance of arrowheads in the cluster. it can be assumed that most actors give and receive emotional support. Thus, the initial stage of analysis indicates that the emotional support network has a social structure similar to the message network divided between givers and takers, with a comparable number of givers exchanging emotional support but far fewer takers receiving any.

Actor Centrality

Freeman Degrees are calculated for all the actors using the binary and valued emotional support matrices. The findings are divided between Tables 3.5 and 3.6 according to the categories of givers and takers derived from the earlier analyses of the message matrix. Comparing the composition of the groups stemming from the message matrix with that of the emotional support matrix shows there is little discrepancy with the givers, and far greater inconsistency with the takers. Only three actors originally grouped with the givers do not provide emotional support to any other member. The takers are consistent in not providing any member with emotional support, but only 26 out of the original 48 receive emotional support. Just one half of the takers are receiving emotional support, whereas 29 out of the original 32 givers are sending and receiving emotional support. Clearly, messages with emotional content are predominantly exchanged among the givers, with relatively little being provided to the takers.

Measures of central tendency for each group's Freeman Degrees further demonstrate this, with the givers sending emotional support to a mean of 8 actors and a median of 7, and receiving it from a mean of 7 and a median of 6 actors. Valued degrees produce a mean of 30 instances of emotional support provided, as well as received by the givers, with corresponding medians of 15 and 20 instances, respectively. In contrast, the takers have no binary outdegrees and receive emotional support from a mean of 1 actor. Valued degrees are not very different: Takers send no instances of emotional support and receive a mean of 2 and median of 1. All the findings based on Freeman Degrees show that a large number of givers are exchanging a great amount of emotional support and giving a bit to the takers, who receive relatively little.

Blockmodeling

A positional or blockmodel analysis is carried out on the emotional support network so that complex relations may be simplified and easily evaluated. To construct blockmodels to describe the presence of emotional support in the established social structure of the SOL-Cancer Forum, the binary and valued emotional

Table 3.5. Freeman Degree Centrality Measures—Binary and Valued Relations of Emotional Support—"Givers"

	Binary Freeman Degrees			Valued Freeman Degrees		
	Outdegree	Indegree	Difference	Outdegree	Indegree	Difference
Elle	42	20	22	198	196	2
Dee	20	13	7	96	56	40
Casey	20	17	3	94	49	45
Murray	20	13	7	82	71	11
Nikki	14	11	3	63	54	9
Breege	13	9	4	49	36	13
Jenn	13	10	3	40	22	18
Robin	12	13	–1	40	46	–6
Helen	11	5	6	29	22	7
GwenQ	10	12	–2	54	62	–8
Tessy	8	6	2	15	12	3
Chad	8	12	–4	9	25	–16
Dudley	7	9	–2	43	49	–6
Joe	7	6	1	26	20	6
NikkiJ	7	5	2	29	26	3
Stella	7	7	0	21	31	–10
Diane	6	7	–1	17	8	9
Marianne	6	5	1	9	19	–10
May	5	9	–4	10	20	–10

(continued)

Table 3.5. *(continued)* Freeman Degree Centrality Measures—Binary and Valued Relations of Emotional Support—"Givers"

	Binary Freeman Degrees			Valued Freeman Degrees		
	Outdegree	Indegree	Difference	Outdegree	Indegree	Difference
Kelly	4	5	–1	12	18	–6
MaryS	3	5	–2	7	20	–13
Lucia	3	6	–3	6	23	–17
FrankieO	3	4	–1	14	18	–4
MargoH	3	6	–3	9	12	–3
Denise	2	2	0	4	3	1
Sophia	1	2	–1	2	3	–1
Jessica	1	2	–1	1	4	–3
Jane	1	1	0	4	5	–1
Amber	1	0	1	2	0	2
Anthony	0	1	–1	0	1	–1
Cracker	0	0	0	0	0	0
No1Fan	0	0	0	0	0	0

Table 3.6. Freeman Degree Centrality Measures—Binary and Valued Relations of Emotional Support—"Takers"

	Binary Freeman Degrees			Valued Freeman Degrees		
	Outdegree	Indegree	Difference	Outdegree	Indegree	Difference
Ron	0	3	–3	0	4	–4
Jennifer	0	3	–3	0	5	–5
Maureen	0	2	–2	0	6	–6
O'Kelly	0	2	–2	0	4	–4
CMD	0	2	–2	0	2	–2
Pen	0	2	–2	0	2	–2
Jamie	0	2	–2	0	3	–3
Stacey	0	1	–1	0	1	–1
Rhea	0	1	–1	0	4	–4
CIGPIC	0	1	–1	0	2	–2
Lorella	0	1	–1	0	1	–1
christina	0	1	–1	0	2	–2
Jan	0	1	–1	0	1	–1
Joan	0	1	–1	0	1	–1
Jose	0	1	–1	0	1	–1
Emily	0	1	–1	0	1	–1
MrsFarm	0	1	–1	0	1	–1
MrsSperi	0	1	–1	0	1	–1
StacyN	0	1	–1	0	1	–1

(continued)

Table 3.6. *(continued)* Freeman Degree Centrality Measures—Binary and Valued Relations of Emotional Support—"Takers"

	Binary Freeman Degrees			Valued Freeman Degrees		
	Outdegree	Indegree	Difference	Outdegree	Indegree	Difference
Violet	0	1	–1	0	1	–1
Ethel	0	1	–1	0	3	–3
Karen	0	1	–1	0	1	–1
Josephine	0	1	–1	0	1	–1
chatnj	0	1	–1	0	2	–2
Vitali	0	1	–1	0	1	–1
Keming	0	1	–1	0	2	–2
RRB	0	0	0	0	0	0
RLBrobook	0	0	0	0	0	0
Rob	0	0	0	0	0	0
Tami	0	0	0	0	0	0
DavidB	0	0	0	0	0	0
Bob	0	0	0	0	0	0
Larry	0	0	0	0	0	0
Helga	0	0	0	0	0	0
Edith	0	0	0	0	0	0
Dkny	0	0	0	0	0	0
Ray	0	0	0	0	0	0
Jeffrey	0	0	0	0	0	0

(continued)

Table 3.6. *(continued)* Freeman Degree Centrality Measures—Binary and Valued Relations of Emotional Support—"Takers"

	Binary Freeman Degrees			Valued Freeman Degrees		
	Outdegree	Indegree	Difference	Outdegree	Indegree	Difference
JuneR	0	0	0	0	0	0
Cathy	0	0	0	0	0	0
MikeK	0	0	0	0	0	0
Ann	0	0	0	0	0	0
MGMLMC	0	0	0	0	0	0
Florence	0	0	0	0	0	0
Tony	0	0	0	0	0	0
Candy	0	0	0	0	0	0
JAT	0	0	0	0	0	0
Conman	0	0	0	0	0	0

support matrices are blocked into two groups based on the partition CONCOR produced for the original message matrix. The densities within and between the givers and the takers are calculated (Tables 3.7 and 3.8), and blockmodels are created using the average density as the cutoff threshold (Figures 3.9 and 3.10).

The densities displayed in Table 3.7 represent the magnitude of members who sent or received a message containing emotional

Table 3.7. Density Table for SOL-Cancer Forum Emotional Support—Binary Data

	1	2
1	0.281	0.023
2	0.000	0.001

Table 3.8. Density Table for SOL-Cancer Forum Emotional Support—Valued Data

	1	2
1	1.191	0.035
2	0.000	0.003

Figure 3.9. Blockmodel image for SOL-Cancer Forum emotional support—binary data

1	**0**
0	**0**

Figure 3.10. Blockmodel image for SOL-Cancer Forum emotional support—valued data

1	**0**
0	**0**

support, both within and between the blocks. The givers (Block 1) have a high density of members transmitting emotional support within their block and a more moderate density when sending it to the takers (Block 2). Conversely, the takers (Block 2) do not engage in providing anyone with emotional support. Indeed, converting the density table to a blockmodel using the average density cutoff of .076 creates an image (Figure 3.9) that suggests a network made up of one clique and the remaining isolates. This characterization persists even when the threshold is half the average density of .038.

Conducting a positional analysis on the valued matrix containing the number of messages sent and received enhances this picture (Table 3.8). The density of the emotional support the givers exchange among themselves increases nearly four times from .281 to 1.191, whereas the emotional support they provide to the takers increases very slightly from .023 to .035. The change in behavior for the takers is nearly nonexistent. Correspondingly, the blockmodel image based on these densities maintains a one-clique pattern whether the threshold is the average density of .307 (Figure 3.10) or half that, .154. These positional analyses confirm that very many of the givers participate in the emotional support network and that they are very active in exchanging this kind of support, mostly to the exclusion of the takers. Hence the kind of support these disperse actors predominantly take from the network does not appear to be emotional in nature.

Informational Support

The sociograms representing the transmission of informational support on the SOL-Cancer Forum (Figures 3.11 and 3.12) are created by graphing the informational support matrices onto the combined support sociogram (Figure 3.6). The most obvious feature of the informational support binary sociogram (Figure 3.11) is its great similarity with that of the combined support sociogram. It displays

Figure 3.11. Sociogram of binary informational support matrix

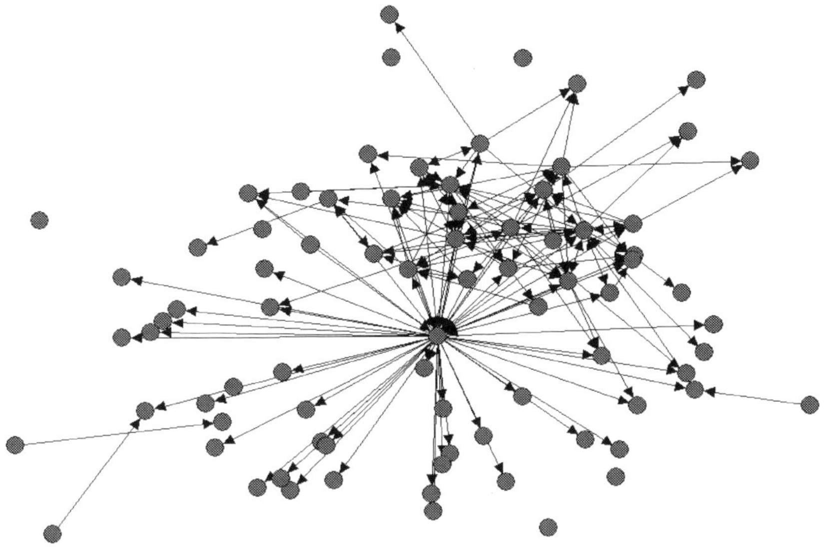

Figure 3.12. Sociogram of valued informational support matrix

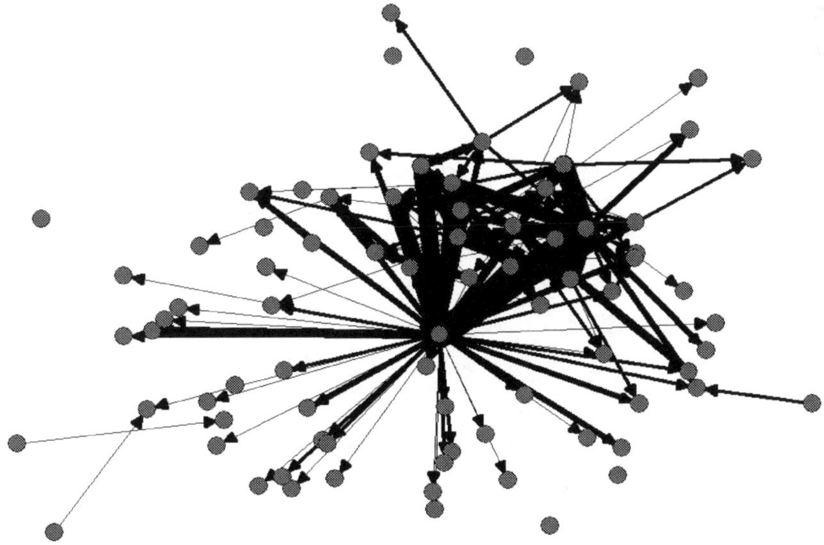

the greatest likeness to the original sociogram of the message matrix (Figure 3.2) when compared with the other two support networks. There is a tight-knit cluster of active members, and nearly all the disperse actors are connected to the network. The informational support network includes the largest number of actors of all the support networks. Nonetheless, the arrowheads indicate that the flow of informational support does maintain the larger pattern of being sent to the takers without being reciprocated.

The valued sociogram (Figure 3.12) indicates the amount of informational support transmitted, represented by the thickness of the lines. The volume of messages sent is typically high for those in the tight-knit cluster but uncommonly large for a number of sparsely connected actors. The takers receive informational support and, in a number of cases, in a fair quantity, unlike other kinds of support. Thus, the two sociograms suggest that although actors in the tight-knit clusters may be the only ones providing informational support, they are not the only ones receiving it. A sizeable number of sparse actors are connected to this network with some receiving more than one instance of informational support.

Actor Centrality

Actor-level Freeman Degrees are calculated to obtain a measure of local centrality by performing the degree command in UCINET 6 on both the binary and valued informational support matrices. The findings presented in Tables 3.9 and 3.10 show that only one actor grouped with the givers does not send or receive informational support and six of the takers do not receive it. In other words, nearly every member of the Forum, 73 out of 80, receives informational support. Comparing the number of takers connected to this network (42) with those in the emotional support (26) and companionship (13) networks demonstrates that informational support is the kind of support they are overwhelmingly taking from the

Table 3.9. Freeman Degree Centrality Measures—Binary and Valued Relations of Informational Support—"Givers"

	Binary Freeman Degrees			Valued Freeman Degrees		
	Outdegree	Indegree	Difference	Outdegree	Indegree	Difference
Elle	51	16	35	116	39	77
Murray	12	9	3	55	22	33
Jenn	11	7	4	29	15	14
Casey	11	2	9	20	5	15
Tessy	9	4	5	22	13	9
Joe	7	2	5	16	4	12
Nikki	7	5	2	9	6	3
Breege	6	4	2	10	12	–2
Robin	6	9	–3	9	20	–11
Dee	6	9	–3	11	20	–9
Stella	6	3	3	11	7	4
May	5	7	–2	10	21	–11
GwenQ	5	3	2	7	6	1
Helen	4	5	–1	6	21	–15
NikkiJ	4	3	1	12	4	8
Jessica	3	2	1	4	4	0
Diane	3	0	3	4	0	4
Chad	3	1	2	3	4	–1
Marianne	2	0	2	3	0	3

(continued)

Table 3.9. *(continued)* Freeman Degree Centrality Measures—Binary and Valued Relations of Informational Support—"Givers"

	Binary Freeman Degrees			Valued Freeman Degrees		
	Outdegree	Indegree	Difference	Outdegree	Indegree	Difference
MargoH	2	4	–2	2	12	–10
Dudley	1	7	–6	3	18	–15
Sophia	1	1	0	1	1	0
MaryS	1	0	1	1	0	1
Jane	1	1	0	3	3	0
Kelly	1	1	0	1	2	–1
Cracker	1	0	1	1	0	1
No1Fan	1	0	1	2	0	2
Amber	1	0	1	1	0	1
Denise	0	1	–1	0	1	–1
Lucia	0	3	–3	0	5	–5
FrankieO	0	2	–2	0	5	–5
Anthony	0	0	0	0	0	0

Table 3.10. Freeman Degree Centrality Measures—Binary and Valued Relations of Informational Support—"Takers"

	Binary Freeman Degrees			Valued Freeman Degrees		
	Outdegree	Indegree	Difference	Outdegree	Indegree	Difference
Ron	0	4	–4	0	8	–8
Joan	0	3	–3	0	4	–4
JuneR	0	3	–3	0	6	–6
StacyN	0	3	–3	0	7	–7
Jennifer	0	3	–3	0	4	–4
Lorella	0	2	–2	0	5	–5
Bob	0	2	–2	0	4	–4
MikeK	0	2	–2	0	3	–3
Ann	0	2	–2	0	2	–2
CMD	0	2	–2	0	6	–6
Pen	0	2	–2	0	4	–4
Keming	0	2	–2	0	4	–4
Stacey	0	1	–1	0	3	–3
RRB	0	1	–1	0	1	–1
RLBrobook	0	1	–1	0	1	–1
Rob	0	1	–1	0	1	–1
Tami	0	1	–1	0	1	–1
christina	0	1	–1	0	2	–2
Jan	0	1	–1	0	1	–1

(continued)

Table 3.10. *(continued)* Freeman Degree Centrality Measures—Binary and Valued Relations of Informational Support—"Takers"

	Binary Freeman Degrees			Valued Freeman Degrees		
	Outdegree	Indegree	Difference	Outdegree	Indegree	Difference
DavidB	0	1	–1	0	1	–1
Larry	0	1	–1	0	1	–1
Helga	0	1	–1	0	1	–1
Edith	0	1	–1	0	1	–1
Dkny	0	1	–1	0	2	–2
Ray	0	1	–1	0	2	–2
Jeffrey	0	1	–1	0	1	–1
Cathy	0	1	–1	0	3	–3
Jose	0	1	–1	0	2	–2
Maureen	0	1	–1	0	1	–1
O'Kelly	0	1	–1	0	1	–1
MGMLMC	0	1	–1	0	1	–1
MrsFarm	0	1	–1	0	1	–1
MrsSperi	0	1	–1	0	2	–2
Ethel	0	1	–1	0	2	–2
Karen	0	1	–1	0	1	–1
Florence	0	1	–1	0	1	–1
Tony	0	1	–1	0	4	–4
Candy	0	1	–1	0	1	–1
Josephine	0	1	–1	0	2	–2

(continued)

Table 3.10. *(continued)* Freeman Degree Centrality Measures—Binary and Valued Relations of Informational Support—"Takers"

	Binary Freeman Degrees			Valued Freeman Degrees		
	Outdegree	Indegree	Difference	Outdegree	Indegree	Difference
JAT	0	1	–1	0	2	–2
Conman	0	1	–1	0	1	–1
Vitali	0	1	–1	0	1	–1
Rhea	0	0	0	0	0	0
CIGPIC	0	0	0	0	0	0
Emily	0	0	0	0	0	0
Violet	0	0	0	0	0	0
chatnj	0	0	0	0	0	0
Jamie	0	0	0	0	0	0

Table 3.11. Total Valued Indegrees for Social Support Networks

	Emotional support	Informational support	Companionship
The givers	931 (95%)	270 (73%)	1,040 (98%)
The takers	54 (5%)	102 (27%)	23 (2%)

Forum. Evaluating the total number of instances of each support the takers receive further supports this notion (Table 3.11). They clearly receive many more instances of informational support than any other kind, twice as many as the next nearest kind, emotional support. In fact, the number of instances the takers amass comprises 27% of all informational support exchanged on the Forum, much more than 5% of emotional support and 2% of companionship. These results also reveal that although this is the kind of support most received by the takers, it is the type least obtained by the givers. The number of instances the givers accrue for informational support is only 270, whereas it is around 1,000 for each of the other two kinds of support. Measures of central tendency for the givers lend further credence to this finding, with the mean and median number of instances sent (12, 4) and received (8, 5) at their lowest when compared with emotional support (30,15) (30,20) and companionship (33,10) (33,12).

The overall Freeman Degrees reveal that the amount of informational support the givers exchange is relatively small, yet almost all of them do participate in the network. In contrast, the takers have the biggest presence and receive the most support in this network. This is clearly the predominant form of support the takers receive. Blockmodels are produced from the information matrices using the message matrix partition of givers and takers to demonstrate that this also holds true at the aggregate level.

Blockmodeling

The blockmodeling technique was used on both the binary (Table 3.12) and valued (Table 3.13) informational support matrices. The densities included in Table 3.12 represent binary ties within and between groups. They demonstrate that the members of the first block provide informational support to other members of their block and, on a smaller scale, to those in the second block. Members of the second block provide no support to those in the first block and just a bit to each other. Applying the mean density cutoff of .051 creates a blockmodel image (Figure 3.13) that denotes a clique with the remaining isolates. However, when the threshold is reduced to one half the average density (.026), the blockmodel (Figure 3.14) becomes one of active members who give to

Table 3.12. Density Table for SOL-Cancer Forum Informational Support—Binary Data

	1	2
1	0.146	0.039
2	0.000	0.018

Table 3.13. Density Table for SOL-Cancer Forum Informational Support—Valued Data

	1	2
1	0.686	0.066
2	0.000	0.023

Figure 3.13. Blockmodel image for SOL-Cancer Forum informational support—binary data

1	**0**
0	**0**

Figure 3.14. Blockmodel image for SOL-Cancer Forum informational support—binary data—one half average density cutoff

1	**1**
0	**0**

themselves and others, and passive members who receive, but do not give to anyone. The presence of the takers remains even in this aggregated and reduced form. In fact, informational support is the single kind of support in which the blockmodel image retains the inclusion of the takers in the network. With all other support networks, even when the mean density cutoff is halved, the blocks representing relationships with the takers are all zeroblocks, and they are classified as isolates.

Applying a blockmodeling technique to the valued informational support matrix shows a much smaller increase in the density within

Figure 3.15. Blockmodel image for SOL-Cancer Forum informational support—valued data

1	**0**
0	**0**

Block 1 than any other form of social support, and a much greater increase in the densities of ties within Block 2, and from Block 1 to Block 2 (Table 3.13). The image formed from these densities (Figure 3.15) does produce a one-clique blockmodel, with both the average density cutoff of .194 and one half that, .097, yet the relative strengths of the densities in blocks relating to the takers demonstrate that informational support is the kind the takers primarily get from the network.

Companionship

The sociogram in Figure 3.16 was created by mapping the binary companionship matrix onto the composite support network configuration. It is the support network that is least similar to the original. As always, there is a tight-knit cluster of actors who share companionship, but there are practically no sparse actors included in this network. The valued sociogram in Figure 3.17

Figure 3.16. Sociogram of binary companionship matrix

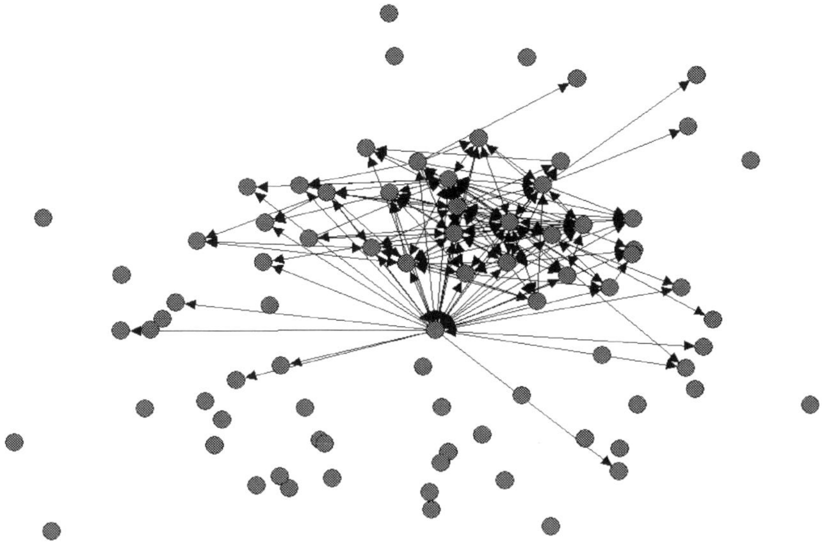

Figure 3.17. Sociogram of valued companionship matrix

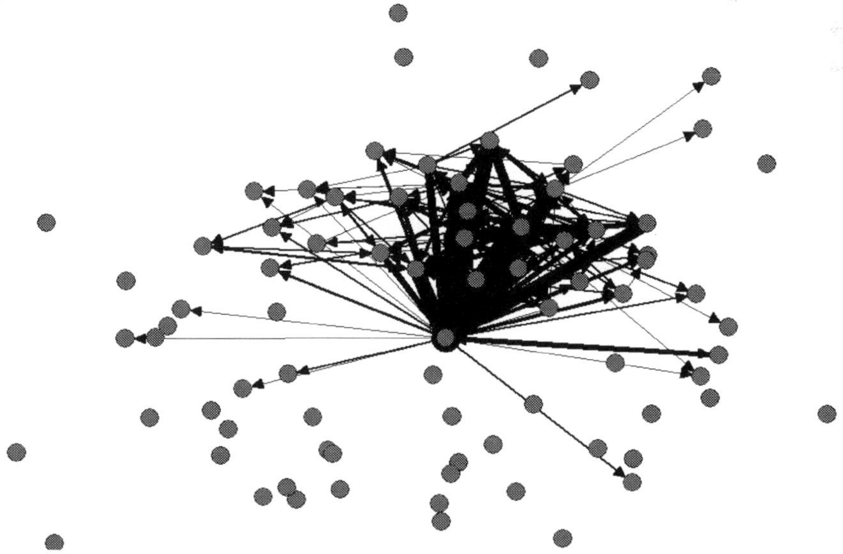

demonstrates that the strength of relationships within the cluster varies and can be very dense. These graphs demonstrate that sparsely connected actors get very little companionship from the Forum, whereas those connected to the tight-knit cluster can be highly active in sending and receiving companionship. It is fitting that those who have more interaction with other members exchange the type of support that extends beyond the explicit subject of the Forum, made up of message content covering topics other than cancer. Those actors who have very little contact with the Forum log on to get information about cancer and do not participate long enough to develop a relationship that extends beyond that.

Actor Centrality

Freeman Degrees are calculated from the companionships matrices using UCINET 6's degree function. The Freeman Degrees for the givers (Table 3.14) reveal that nearly all (29) members of the original group are included in the companionship network, whereas only 13 of the takers receive companionship, just over a quarter of the group (Table 3.15). This is the smallest group of takers included in any of the support networks, buttressing the notion that most of the takers do not receive companionship from the network. The givers, on the other hand, are very active in exchanging companionship. The valued degrees show the very large number of instances of companionship that they send and receive, ranging from 1 to 281,[22] and from 2 to 255. Measures of central tendency produce a mean number of 33 instances sent and received for both binary and valued relations, with medians of 10 and 12, respectively. In addition, reviewing the total number of instances sent and received by the givers in each category of support (Table 3.11) illustrates that givers receive 1,040 instances of companionship from one another compared with 931

Table 3.14. Freeman Degree Centrality Measures—Binary and Valued Relations of Companionship—“Givers”

	Binary Freeman Degrees			Valued Freeman Degrees		
	Outdegree	Indegree	Difference	Outdegree	Indegree	Difference
Elle	33	20	13	281	255	26
Casey	23	16	7	167	113	54
Dee	19	14	5	84	85	–1
Breege	13	11	2	41	41	0
Jenn	11	12	–1	66	61	5
Chad	11	10	1	34	36	–2
Murray	10	10	0	43	44	–1
Nikki	10	10	0	75	37	38
Helen	9	3	6	26	17	9
GwenQ	8	7	1	32	31	1
Robin	7	9	–2	42	50	–8
Stella	6	7	–1	29	41	–12
MargoH	6	4	2	12	8	4
Joe	5	6	–1	48	58	–10
Dudley	5	8	–3	6	26	–20
May	5	5	0	12	11	1
Kelly	5	3	2	10	10	0
NikkiJ	4	7	–3	16	22	–6
Diane	4	6	–2	6	20	–14

(continued)

Table 3.14. *(continued)* Freeman Degree Centrality Measures—Binary and Valued Relations of Companionship—"Givers"

	Binary Freeman Degrees			Valued Freeman Degrees		
	Outdegree	Indegree	Difference	Outdegree	Indegree	Difference
Jessica	4	4	0	8	11	–3
Tessy	3	4	–1	8	11	–3
FrankieO	2	4	–2	4	12	–8
Denise	2	3	–1	4	8	–4
MaryS	2	3	–1	3	3	0
Marianne	2	1	1	2	2	0
Lucia	1	3	–2	1	9	–8
Jane	1	1	0	1	9	–8
Anthony	1	3	–2	2	4	–2
Sophia	0	2	–2	0	5	–5
Cracker	0	0	0	0	0	0
No1Fan	0	0	0	0	0	0
Amber	0	0	0	0	0	0

Table 3.15. Freeman Degree Centrality Measures—Binary and Valued Relations of Companionship—"Takers"

	Binary Freeman Degrees			Valued Freeman Degrees		
	Outdegree	Indegree	Difference	Outdegree	Indegree	Difference
Karen	0	2	–2	0	6	–6
Ron	0	2	–2	0	2	–2
CMD	0	2	–2	0	2	–2
Rhea	0	1	–1	0	2	–2
MrsSperi	0	1	–1	0	2	–2
Jennifer	0	1	–1	0	2	–2
JuneR	0	1	–1	0	1	–1
Maureen	0	1	–1	0	1	–1
MrsFarm	0	1	–1	0	1	–1
Violet	0	1	–1	0	1	–1
JAT	0	1	–1	0	1	–1
Vitali	0	1	–1	0	1	–1
Keming	0	1	–1	0	1	–1
Stacey	0	0	0	0	0	0
CIGPIC	0	0	0	0	0	0
RRB	0	0	0	0	0	0
Lorella	0	0	0	0	0	0
RLBrobook	0	0	0	0	0	0
Rob	0	0	0	0	0	0

(continued)

Table 3.15. *(continued)* Freeman Degree Centrality Measures—Binary and Valued Relations of Companionship—“Takers”

	Binary Freeman Degrees			Valued Freeman Degrees		
	Outdegree	Indegree	Difference	Outdegree	Indegree	Difference
Tami	0	0	0	0	0	0
christina	0	0	0	0	0	0
Jan	0	0	0	0	0	0
DavidB	0	0	0	0	0	0
Bob	0	0	0	0	0	0
Larry	0	0	0	0	0	0
Helga	0	0	0	0	0	0
Edith	0	0	0	0	0	0
Dkny	0	0	0	0	0	0
Ray	0	0	0	0	0	0
Joan	0	0	0	0	0	0
Jeffrey	0	0	0	0	0	0
Cathy	0	0	0	0	0	0
Jose	0	0	0	0	0	0
Emily	0	0	0	0	0	0
MikeK	0	0	0	0	0	0
Ann	0	0	0	0	0	0
O’Kelly	0	0	0	0	0	0
MGMLMC	0	0	0	0	0	0
StacyN	0	0	0	0	0	0

(continued)

Table 3.15. *(continued)* Freeman Degree Centrality Measures—Binary and Valued Relations of Companionship—"Takers"

	Binary Freeman Degrees			Valued Freeman Degrees		
	Outdegree	Indegree	Difference	Outdegree	Indegree	Difference
Pen	0	0	0	0	0	0
Ethel	0	0	0	0	0	0
Florence	0	0	0	0	0	0
Tony	0	0	0	0	0	0
Candy	0	0	0	0	0	0
Josephine	0	0	0	0	0	0
chatnj	0	0	0	0	0	0
Conman	0	0	0	0	0	0
Jamie	0	0	0	0	0	0

of emotional support and 270 of information. In contrast, takers only receive 23 instances of companionship, much fewer than both emotional support (54) and informational support (102). The Freeman Degrees support the observation that the givers participate greatly in the transmission of companionship to the relative exclusion of the takers. Blockmodeling reveals that this pattern holds true when the actors are aggregated into the two groups before the analysis.

Blockmodeling

The positional analysis is conducted on the companionship matrix using CONCOR partitions of givers and takers derived from the message matrix. Grouping the actors according to the social structure found in the message network allows an analysis of the relationship between the structure and the transmission of companionship. The binary density table (Table 3.16) demonstrates that actors in Block 1 have ties to a fair number of members within their own block and a very sparse relation with

Table 3.16. Density Table for SOL-Cancer Forum Companionship—Binary Data

	1	2
1	0.249	0.011
2	0.000	0.002

Table 3.17. Density Table for SOL-Cancer Forum Companionship—Valued Data

	1	2
1	1.465	0.016
2	0.000	0.003

Figure 3.18. Blockmodel image for SOL-Cancer Forum Companionship—binary data

1	0
0	0

those in Block 2. Those in Block 2 have no ties within their own block or with Block 1. The blockmodel image created using the average density cutoff of .065 illustrates a one-clique network (Figure 3.18). Using one half the average density cutoff of .033 would not change this result. The givers are providing each other with companionship, but the takers are not at all included in the network.

The valued density table (Table 3.17) and blockmodel image (Figure 3.19) maintain this one-clique structure, but the addition

Figure 3.19. Blockmodel image for SOL-Cancer Forum Companionship—valued data

1	0
0	0

of the number of messages sent reveals the intensity of relationships within Block 1. The density within that block is much greater than for any other kind of support, 1.465 compared with 1.191 for emotional support and .686 for informational support. Clearly, companionship makes up the greatest portion of all the support the givers send to one another and is the kind of support the takers receive the least.

Conclusion

The structure of the SOL-Cancer Forum can broadly be described as made up of two categories of actors: the givers and the takers.

The first group contains actors who both give and receive support, whereas the second only takes support without reciprocating. A network sociogram graphically displayed the initial insight into the bifurcated nature of the network, which was then substantiated by the highly differentiated network centralization indexes. A small centralization outdegree index revealed a lesser number of actors are sending messages than are receiving them as was suggested by a large centralization indegree index. The existence of two divergent positions was further substantiated at the actor level, with members' outdegrees demonstrating a clear distinction between those actors who sent a message to at least one other member and those who did not send any directed messages at all. Finally, a blockmodel established the pattern of relations between the two positions by demonstrating the density of ties from the givers to the takers and conversely the scarcity of ties from the takers to the givers.

The transmission of social support within the network structure showed a general pattern of those who contributed to the Forum receiving the greatest diversity and extent of support from the Forum. The givers both gave and received all three kinds of support in varying amounts, whereas the takers predominantly only received informational support and to a lesser degree than the givers. Clearly, members' interactions on the Forum both construct the social structure of the group and influence the transmission of social support within it. Actors who send messages to one another become part of a group in which members support each other in every way they can. Those who do not interact with other members are not integrated into the group, and although they can receive some support from it, the amount is circumscribed and the form tends to be limited to informational support.

All the findings describing the broad structure of SOL-Cancer Forum clearly demonstrate that the takers display consistently uniform activity, whereas the givers engage in a wide range of varied behaviors. As such, any additional analyses of message sending by the takers will not yield new findings, whereas the complexity of activity demonstrated by the givers demands further exploration. The next chapter moves the analysis deeper into the network and examines the intricate social structure created by the givers' diverse participation and its effect on social support.

CHAPTER 4

A NETWORK OF SOLERS AND THEIR STAR

The previous chapter demonstrated the broadly bifurcated nature of the SOL-Cancer Forum's network and its effect on the transmission of social support. Actors are categorized as occupying the position of givers, who supply each other and the takers with support, or takers, who do not provide anyone with support. In addition to revealing the uniform behavior of the takers, an initial glimpse of the varied and complex activity of the givers is presented. The current chapter advances the analysis into the intricate social structure created by the givers' diverse participation, providing a more comprehensive description of members' patterns of interaction and their effects on social support.

THE GIVERS

The valued message matrix sociogram presented in the previous chapter (Figure 3.2) provides the first indication of the network configuration of the givers in the Forum. Generally, they appear to constitute a large cluster of actors who are highly interconnected. More precisely, some of these actors seem to be more centrally located and highly connected with very thick lines, whereas others seem to be somewhat more peripherally located and loosely connected by thinner lines. There is also one giver who stands out from the rest. This actor is undoubtedly one of the givers, however she is also connected to many more disperse actors than any other giver and occupies the most central position in the network. In sum, this sociogram suggests that the givers engage in a wide range of online activities that vary by how much contact they make and who they make contact with.

A NETWORK OF SOLERS

The visual representation of the Forum's interactions presented in the valued message matrix sociogram (Figure 3.2) displays three distinct features of the network: a central actor; the disperse actors connected to her; and a cluster of highly active tightly-knit actors. The disperse actors behave uniformly as takers of support and are therefore excluded from the group of givers. This is not the case with the central actor and those in the tight-knit cluster, who engage in a great variety of supportive behaviors. These actors are regular members of the Forum, consider the group a family, and refer to themselves as the SOLers. They defer to the central actor as their leader, but her role is not the only discernible or significant one within the group. Among the SOLers there are a number of distinct positions and relations between them. To identify actors' positions in the network, SOLers' Freeman Degrees are examined, followed by a core/periphery model[23] to confirm the accuracy of these positions and to describe the roles they play in the network.

Actor Centrality

The configuration of the network displayed in the valued message matrix sociogram (Figure 3.2) demonstrates the important role centrality plays in generating the distinct structural features of the network. Large divisions in the network result from three features: one node having a strong degree of centrality in relation to all other actors; a concentrated cluster of actors sharing a strong degree of centralization among themselves; and a region of greatly dispersed actors on the outskirts of the network possessing low centrality. The sociogram offers an initial glimpse of network centrality but cannot provide an in-depth analysis of each member's behavior that determines their position in the social structure. Freeman Degrees, on the other hand, offer a very precise measure of each actor's local centrality based on message sending and receiving, which reveals their network position.

The valued and binary Freeman outdegrees and indegrees for the SOLers are presented in Table 4.1. The entries in the first two columns display valued Freeman Degrees that reflect the number of messages sent and received. The range of degrees provides an indication of how varied the SOLers behavior is, extending from 1 to 200 messages sent, and from 0 to 187 received. Turning to the binary Freeman Degrees, that is, the number of actors each SOLer sent at least one message to and received at least one message from, further reveals the SOLers' diversity, ranging from 1 to 69, and 0 to 23, respectively. The actors' degrees are used to sort the SOLers into four categories according to the levels of activity, which establish the actors' positions in the network. The four categories are presented in Table 4.1 and described in the following sections, beginning with the network star and moving sequentially through the remaining categories.

Table 4.1. Freeman Degree Centrality Measures —Valued and Binary Message Matrices Including Categorical Cutpoints

	Valued Freeman Degrees			Binary Freeman Degrees		
	Outdegree	Indegree	Difference	Outdegree	Indegree	Difference
Elle	200	187	13	69	23	46
			Cutpoint—prime givers			
Casey	127	80	47	28	20	8
Murray	77	59	18	21	17	4
Dee	64	49	15	24	15	9
Jenn	59	42	17	19	16	3
Nikki	50	35	15	15	12	3
Robin	44	48	–4	15	16	–1
			Cutpoint—serious members			
Joe	30	29	1	9	7	2
Breege	29	27	2	15	12	3
GwenQ	29	33	–4	11	12	–1
Helen	24	18	6	11	5	6
Stella	23	25	–2	10	8	2
NikkiJ	20	20	0	8	8	0
Tessy	18	12	6	11	8	3
May	17	24	–7	9	10	–1
Dudley	15	19	–4	8	9	–1
Chad	15	20	–5	11	13	–2

(continued)

Table 4.1.*(continued)* Freeman Degree Centrality Measures —Valued and Binary Message Matrices Including Categorical Cutpoints

	Valued Freeman Degrees			Binary Freeman Degrees		
	Outdegree	Indegree	Difference	Outdegree	Indegree	Difference
			Cutpoint—moderate users			
Kelly	10	11	−1	6	5	1
MargoH	9	11	−2	6	7	−1
Jessica	8	10	−2	5	5	0
Diane	8	16	−8	8	9	−1
Marianne	7	7	0	6	5	1
FrankieO	7	10	−3	3	4	−1
Jane	5	4	1	2	2	0
MaryS	4	8	−4	3	5	−2
Denise	3	5	−2	3	4	−1
Lucia	3	11	−8	3	6	−3
Sophia	1	5	−4	1	4	−3
Cracker	1	0	1	1	0	1
No1Fan	1	0	1	1	0	1
Anthony	1	3	−2	1	3	−2
Amber	1	0	1	1	0	1
			Cutpoint—support takers			

The Network Star

The most glaring phenomenon in Table 4.1 is the disproportionately high level of activity exhibited by the central actor, Elle, both in the number of actors she is in contact with and the volume of messages she sends. Elle's binary outdegree reveals that she has sent at least one message to 69 out of the 79 other members in the network. Meanwhile, Casey, who is the second most active member, only contacted 28 members, a difference of 41 actors. The valued outdegrees suggest a greater discrepancy as Elle sends out 200 messages in the two-week period, compared with Casey's 127. Casey has also sent out a large volume of messages, which becomes more evident when comparing with the mean number of messages sent by the givers (28). Nonetheless, she is still no match for Elle, whose total number of messages sent is 73 more than hers. Elle clearly displays an exceptional position of dominance that cannot be matched with any other actor and, therefore, is placed in a unique category as the network star.

Elle's binary indegree establishes her primacy in receiving messages because she collects them from the greatest number of members (23). Notably, however, this is only 3 more than Casey and 15 more than the group mean of 8. These smaller differences are in great contrast with her binary outdegree of 69 in comparison with a group mean of 11. Thus, although she does lead the group in both the number of members she sends to and the number she receives from, the great volume of actors she sends to is much more distinct. She clearly posts messages to many more members than she collects from. This is illustrated in the lower half of the valued message matrix sociogram (Figure 3.2), where Elle has lines connecting her to a great number of members, with arrowheads that only point away from her. All in all, Elle's binary outdegree and indegree demonstrate her central role in the network as the actor with connections to the greatest number of nodes. She is also principally responsible for connecting the support takers to the rest of network by doing most of the work in sending messages to them even though they do not send any direct messages back.

Elle's binary indegree may not seem large enough to represent a dominant node, but a review of her valued indegree dispels any doubt. The 23 members who contacted her sent a total of 187 messages. Once again, Casey, the next nearest actor, falls short, with 80 messages received from 20 members. Likewise, the mean number of messages received by the givers is 36, five times less than the number Elle receives. Furthermore, the difference between the number of messages Elle sent and received is only 13, which is much smaller than the difference between the number of actors she sent to and received from (46). As such, her valued indegree demonstrates the focal position she occupies among the givers, reflected in the very large volume of directed message she receives from a much smaller number of actors.

All these findings not only establish Elle as the center of the network but also the leader. She receives the greatest number of messages, from the largest number of members, who send her an average of eight messages each. Elle, likewise, sends the greatest number of messages, to the largest number of members, and, as any leader should, responds to nearly all those who post, often being the only member who sends a message to some actors (28). A brief analysis of messages posted to the Forum lends further credence to Elle's role as the unofficial leader. Veteran SOLers extol Elle's extraordinary dedication to the Forum: Jane declares, "You are the heart of this group"; Robin exclaims, "once again 'Superlady' to the rescue!"; and GwenQ gushes,

> Elle, You are amazing my friend! I can tell from Helen's mail that she is worried on many levels and here you are, trying to help her on all of them. Darn, I'm sitting here tearing up just realizing once again how special you are to each of us. Love you much Elle... GwenQ

Even new members quickly notice her dominate role. Helen's third post to the Forum begins, "Hi Elle and everyone else out there!" After a few exchanges with members on the group, Dudley asks Elle, "Are you the moderator?"; and in her second week of membership, Breege pronounces, "It's no wonder you are such a focal point of this forum." There are also numerous accounts of Elle being referred to as an individual's or the group's guardian angel, not to mention "a gift from God to us all."

It is not surprising that the actor who empirically occupies the center of a network is also perceived as the leader by those in the network. Freeman, Roeder, and Mulholland (1979) found an association between leadership and centrality when replicating an earlier MIT experiment on structural centrality. "[T]he MIT experiment was designed to study the effects of the structure of communication—or, specifically, the centrality of points in the communication structure—on problem solving, perception of leadership and personal satisfaction" (p. 121). In keeping with the previous experiment, Freeman et al. (1979) sought to illuminate communication patterns in small groups by conducting a number of communication exercises in which participants could only interact by passing notes through a slot. Following the exercises, each subject was given a questionnaire to fill out. The authors found that when members of each group were asked to nominate a leader if they felt there was one, the actor who was central in regard to communication patterns was also nominated as the leader in most cases.

The SOLers

Even though the remaining members of the givers do not demonstrate the exceptional participation of the star actor, they do display a wide range of message-sending activity, quite unlike the uniformity of behavior exhibited by the takers. The valued

Freeman Degrees are used to sort the SOLers into four categories according to level of activity (Table 4.1) to gain explanatory power over their varied participation and produce a more straightforward representation of their interactions. These categories distinguish the actors' positions in the network, which can then be analyzed to uncover the patterns of interactions between them to construct the Forum's social structure. The ranges of binary and valued degrees for the actors in each category are presented in Table 4.2 to provide a more nuanced account of behavior.

The first category is solely occupied by Elle, the star, on account of her unambiguous position of dominance in both sending and receiving messages. Moving out from the star, the second category contains a small group of prime givers (6) who send and receive the second largest number of messages, from 44 to127 and 35 to 80, respectively (Table 4.2). These SOLers are classified as prime givers because, as demonstrated by their valued degrees, they send out many more messages than they receive and a much greater number of messages than all others, apart from Elle. In addition, according to their binary degrees, they also send messages to three to nine more members than they receive from.[24] The next category is made up of 10 serious members who

Table 4.2. Freeman Degree Centrality Measures—Valued and Binary Message Matrices—Four SOLer Categories

	Valued Freeman Degrees		Binary Freeman Degrees	
	Outdegree	Indegree	Outdegree	Indegree
Star	200	187	69	23
Prime givers	44–127	35–80	15–28	12–20
Serious members	15–30	12–33	8–15	5–13
Moderate users	1–10	0–16	1–8	0–9

send and receive a fair number of messages, anywhere from 15 to 30 sent and 12 to 33 received. The number of actors they made contact with (8 to 15) and who contacted them (5 to 13) varies between the extremes of one serious member sending messages to 6 more individuals than she receives from and another sending to 2 fewer than he receives from (Table 4.1). The final group contains 15 moderate users who send between 1 and 10 messages and receive from 0 to 16. Even though one member of this group receives a fair number of messages at 16, the mean for this category is 7. Moderate users on the whole send and receive fewer messages than do the other SOLers, well below the means of the entire group of SOLers at 28 sent and 26 received. Moderate users' binary degrees reveal they tend to receive messages from roughly the same number of actors they send to, ranging from 1 to 8 and 0 to 9, respectively. The actors' positions in relation to the entire network structure will be evaluated using a core periphery procedure to confirm the accuracy and reliability of these classifications when moving from the local level to the system level. This measure will also provide insight into the centrality of relations in the network by revealing if the network has a core, the category or categories of actors that make up the core, and the relationship of all other categories to it.

Network Centrality

A continuous core periphery model was created using UCINET 6 on the valued message matrix with all isolates removed to identify the SOLers patterns of behavior in relation to the center of the network and to verify the four classifications based on Freeman Degrees. The continuous model is employed in lieu of a basic core periphery model to provide a more nuanced description of actors' positions and their relations, rather than just the two categories of core and periphery and the binary relationship they imply (Borgatti

& Everett, 1999). The sociograms display a star configuration and the Freeman Degrees demonstrate the dominance of one central actor in message sending and receiving. This makes it necessary to employ an accurate and reliable measure designed specifically to determine whether a network has a center, the actor or actors who comprise it, and the nature of the remaining actors' relationship to it. This measure is also used to buttress findings based on Freeman Degrees because "[t]he coreness measure is only interpretable to the extent that the model fits, (whereas) a centrality measure is interpretable no matter what the structure of the network" (Borgatti & Everett, 1999, p. 392).

A correlation coefficient of .929 signifies a good fit between the model and the ideal pattern matrix. As such, the resulting coreness measures suitably represent the continuous core periphery structure of the network. The model results in each actor receiving a number representing his or her measure of coreness, that is, how close each actor is to the core of the network (Table 4.3). Elle is established as the innermost core of the network because she possesses the greatest coreness value of .790, and the procedure recommends a core size of 1. The large disparity between the value she receives and the next nearest member (.485) further substantiates her position as the network star.

The second Freeman Degree classification of prime givers is similarly supported by coreness values. All six of these actors are grouped together and have coreness measures that situate them closest to the center, moving outward consecutively. Moreover, calculating the continuous coreness model with the star actor removed, that is, all ties to or from Elle eliminated from the matrix, results in the recommended core being made up of these six actors.[25] There is general agreement between the coreness values and the Freeman Degree categorization for the next category of serious members, with the exception of three actors. Two actors

Table 4.3. Coreness Measures of Valued Message Matrix Including Coreness Cutpoints

	Measure of coreness	Difference between measures of coreness
Elle	0.790	0.485
	Cutpoint—prime givers	
Casey	0.305	0.054
Murray	0.251	0.049
Robin	0.202	0.023
Dee	0.179	0.008
Nikki	0.171	0.007
Jenn	0.164	0.035
	Cutpoint—serious members	
Joe	0.129	0.013
GwenQ	0.116	0.013
Stella	0.103	0.009
Helen	0.094	0.022
May	0.072	0.004
NikkiJ	0.068	0.006
Diane	0.062	0.006
Dudley	0.056	0.000
Jessica	0.056	0.007
Tessy	0.049	0.000
Breege	0.049	0.004
	Cutpoint—moderate users	
Lucia	0.045	0.000
FrankieO	0.045	0.011
Chad	0.034	0.002
Jane	0.032	0.000
Kelly	0.032	0.001
MargoH	0.031	0.004
Karen	0.027	0.005
Marianne	0.022	0.004
	Cutpoint—takers	

now classified as serious members were previously grouped with the moderate users, and another actor is now placed with the moderate users instead of the serious members. It appears that this is the level of activity at which actor location in relation to the center of the network and actor degree, or simple posting activity, start to decouple. In fact, for the last category, moderate users, there is agreement with only 6 of the 15 actors. This is because of the fact that, unlike individual Freeman Degrees, coreness values do not reveal how connected an actor is to anyone but how connected an actor is to the core of the network.

A UCINET autocorrelation ANOVA/Density procedure is used to test the significance of the categories in relation to the center, given the slight discrepancy found when moving to the farthest reaches of the categories created using Freeman Degrees. Using the structural blockmodel technique of this procedure indicates a good model fit with a significant R^2 of .827. Each of the four categories also exhibits a significant density of ties from their group to the core actor and vice versa. This confirms that the actors grouped in each category demonstrate a significant patterned relationship with the core of the network. The categories of serious members and moderate users are also supported by a substantive understanding of the data. Reviewing the posting behavior of actors who make up the serious members confirms they all share the characteristic of consistently contributing a fair number of messages to the Forum and steadily receiving them as well. This can be said for the sample period and beyond. There is some variance in the number of messages they send and receive; however, their overall pattern of interaction is parallel and, for purposes of data reduction, well-suited to being represented by one category. The same can be said for the actors categorized as moderate users, who are all return posters and receive directed messages, but to a much lesser degree than do the serious members.

THE SOCIAL STRUCTURE OF THE SOL-CANCER FORUM

The network's social structure can be understood with "the subsequent appraisal of the relations connecting positions to one another" (Knoke & Kuklinski, 1982, p. 18), now that the actors' positions in a network and the relations among them have been identified. To do so, initially a collapsed valued message matrix was created by summing the number of messages sent by the actors in each category, yielding one total for each grouping (Table 4.4). This collapsed valued matrix can now be subjected to a number of network analytic procedures to reveal the social structure of the SOL-Cancer Forum, first through a graphic representation of the matrix in the form of a sociogram (Figure 4.1). The takers are included in the collapsed matrix, the sociogram, and all further analyses because the Forum's entire social structure will be described.

The collapsed sociogram demonstrates the give-and-take nature of the SOLers' relationships, with each of the four categories displaying three inward facing arrowheads, indicating that every SOLer category sends messages to every other. The varying thickness of the lines connecting categories, however, suggests the relationships are not all equivalent. There is a general pattern of every SOLer category providing some support messages, but the exchange is

Table 4.4. Collapsed Message Matrix—Valued—Five Categories

	Star	Prime givers	Serious members	Moderate users	Takers
Star	0	63	60	30	47
Prime givers	112	141	101	50	17
Serious members	61	77	56	15	11
Moderate users	14	32	10	6	7
Takers	0	0	0	0	0

Figure 4.1. Sociogram of collapsed message matrix

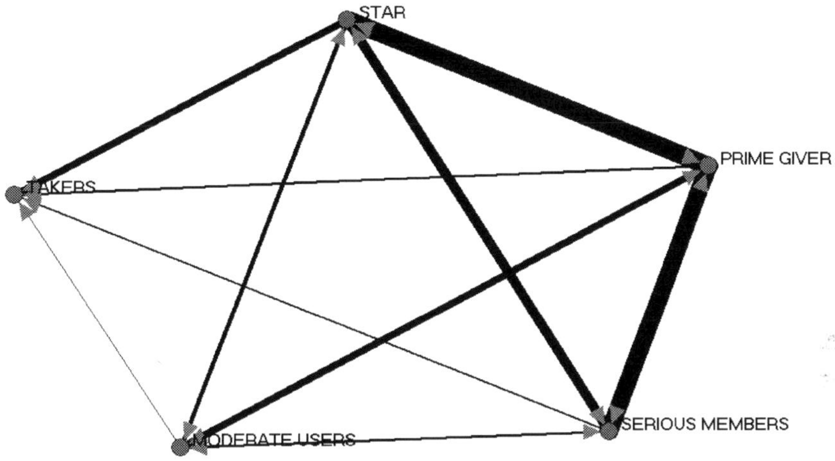

not always reciprocal. The role that each SOLer category plays in the uneven distribution of support messages is also evident in the matrix. The number of messages sent shows that the star maintains a position of supremacy in sending to the takers, yet in other categories her dominance is surpassed. It is important to keep in mind that she is only one actor, whereas the other SOLer categories contain anywhere from 6 to 15 members. Nonetheless, the configuration of the collapsed sociogram (Figure 4.1) similarly reveals that in this form the network is no longer dominated by one central node. The star's attenuated position as the core actor is easily observable when comparing the network sociogram based on the original message matrix (Figure 3.1) with the collapsed sociogram.

Collapsing the actors into categories not only reveals the diminished primacy of the star but also allows the role of the prime givers to be discerned. The prime givers are the only actors who send more messages to the star than they receive from her. She exchanges about the same number of messages with the serious members, sends twice as much to the moderate users, and sends a great amount to the takers without receiving any. The prime givers, however, send her 49 more messages than they receive from her. This is nearly the number of messages she sends to the takers, who send nothing in response. It appears that while the star is doing all the work in supporting the takers, the prime givers are the members who are compensating and supporting her. Furthermore, the prime givers are the sole category that sends more messages to every other group than they receive. They also exchange a much larger number of messages with one another than they send out to the others. Overall, this category truly is made up of prime givers who are second only to the star in supporting the rest of the SOLers and stand out in supporting themselves.

As for the last two categories of SOLers, the serious members tend to contribute to the network and support themselves. With the exception of the prime givers, the serious members generally transmit about the same number of messages to the other SOLers as they collect from them. They also send one another a total of 56 messages, which is relatively close to the number of messages they send to those they have the most active relationships with, the star (61) and the prime givers (77). The moderate users, on the other hand, take much more from the network than they contribute. They receive anywhere from 5 to 18 more messages from the other SOLers than they send to them, and they exchange fewer messages with each other than the number of messages any of the other SOLers send them.

The SOLers' Supportive Roles

Applying a blockmodeling technique to assess these supportive roles confirms this characterization. Given the variable amounts of support provided by the four SOLer categories, before creating a blockmodel it is first necessary to establish which categories supply others with a surplus of support messages above what they receive. A surplus support message matrix is created using a three-step process. Initially

UCINET 6 is used to create a density matrix that represents the densities of messages sent between and within categories (Table 4.5). This matrix is then used to create a minimum density matrix where each cell contains the smaller value for each pair of categories, that is, cells *ij* and *ji* are both replaced by the smaller value of the two. Next, the minimum density matrix is subtracted from the original density matrix, resulting in a surplus support message density matrix where each cell contains either the surplus amount of support messages when the sending category provides the receiving category with a greater density of ties, or a zero when they provide the other category with a smaller density of ties (Table 4.6).

Table 4.5. Density Matrix of Collapsed Message Matrix—Five Categories

	Star	Prime givers	Serious members	Moderate users	Takers
Star		10.500	6.000	2.000	0.979
Prime givers	18.667	4.700	1.683	0.556	0.059
Serious members	6.100	1.283	0.622	0.100	0.023
Moderate users	0.933	0.356	0.067	0.029	0.010
Takers	0	0	0	0	0

Table 4.6. Surplus Support Message Density Table of Collapsed Message Matrix

	Star	Prime givers	Serious members	Moderate users	Takers
Star		0	0	1.067	0.979
Prime givers	8.167		0.400	0.200	0.059
Serious members	0.100	0		0.033	0.023
Moderate users	0	0	0		0.010
Takers	0	0	0	0	

These findings reveal the categories of actors that provide a surplus of support messages and the amount of excess support provided. It is now possible to create a blockmodel (Table 4.7) and a reduced sociogram (Figure 4.2) reflecting those relationships. The average density cutoff value of 0.552 is applied to the surplus support message density table to produce the blockmodel matrix, which is then used to create the reduced sociogram. Both the blockmodel and the reduced sociogram display a structure of sending support messages similar to that suggested by the collapsed message matrix but not identical.

The star no longer uniquely occupies a position of primacy because she is now supported by the prime givers. The serious members are in a position of independence in relation to the surplus support message network because of their pattern of giving and receiving equitable amounts, which leaves them debt-free. Both the moderate users and the takers emerge as appropriators of support messages who do not adequately reciprocate. The disparity between the structure suggested by the surplus blockmodel (Table 4.7) and that of the collapsed message matrix (Table 4.4) stems from the question of network dominance. The collapsed message matrix presents the prime givers as occupying

Table 4.7. Surplus Support Message Blockmodel of Collapsed Message Matrix

	Star	Prime givers	Serious members	Moderate users	Takers
Star		0	0	1	1
Prime givers	1		0	0	0
Serious members	0	0		0	0
Moderate users	0	0	0		0
Takers	0	0	0	0	

Figure 4.2. Reduced sociogram for surplus support message blockmodel of collapsed message matrix

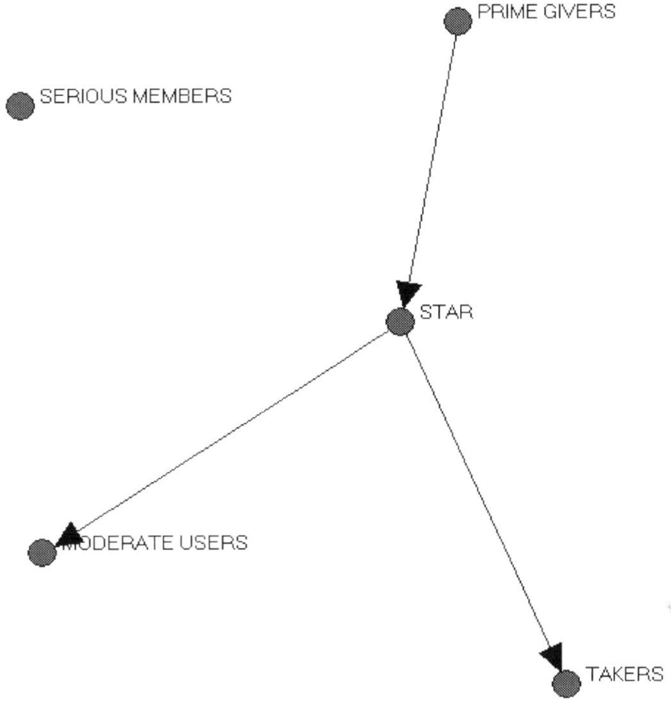

the principal role in sending the greatest number of messages to all other SOLers, whereas the star only leads in sending to the takers. On the other hand, the surplus support message blockmodel identifies the star as responsible for supporting two of the remaining four categories, both the moderate users and the takers, and places her back in the center of the surplus support message network. The prime givers maintain their position as supports of the star, but with the serious users no longer indebted to any group, she is the only category they provide with surplus support messages.

One possible method of adjudicating the ambiguity in network dominance is to review the collapsed density matrix (Table 4.5) because it offers a measure of message sending that takes category size into account, unlike the raw counts presented in the collapsed message matrix (Table 4.4), which do not. After all, the star is only one actor, whereas the prime givers are six. The collapsed density matrix suggests that even though the actually number of messages the star sends to the other three SOLer categories is smaller compared with the prime givers, when you account for the size of each category, her message-sending activity appears to be more dense than that of the prime givers for every category. This measure then places the star back in a position of dominance over the prime givers, as well as the other categories. Nonetheless, comparing these densities is not completely appropriate; while it is significant that the star is a lone actor who sends an enormous number of messages, surpassed only by the activity of six actors combined, comparing the densities of a group of actors' behaviors with that of one actor does have flaws.

These contradictory findings question the nature and extent of the star actor's dominant role. She could fulfill the unique role of principally sustaining the entire network such that if she were to leave the Forum another actor would need to emerge as the star or the network would fall apart. On the other hand, Elle's role as the central actor may be sustained by the sheer volume of activity, in which case, if she were to leave, the six prime givers could carry on in her place and maintain the network. A number of analyses are carried out on a matrix with the star actor removed, that is, all ties to and from Elle eliminated from the matrix, to probe these prospects.

Simply creating this matrix reveals the unique role that Elle plays in sending support messages to a great many actors whom no other member interacts with. Removing all the messages she sent results in more than half of the takers (28) becoming isolates and dropping out of the network. Calculating the network centralization without the star actor also demonstrates this because the outdegree centralization index decreases greatly from 83% with Elle to 45% without her. The decrease in outdegree centralization shows message sending no longer originates from as concentrated a center as it did when Elle was included, thus revealing the amount of concentration in message sending that stemmed exclusively from her activity. Furthermore, the increase in the indegree index, from 24% to 29%, although slight, confirms the number of actors Elle is solely responsible for contacting. Along with Elle, a great many takers who are cutoff from the network without her messages are not included in the matrix when calculating the network centralization.[26] If these actors remained in the network by virtue of being connected to other members, there would have been an even greater diffusion of actors receiving messages than in the original network, resulting in a decrease in the indegree centralization index. The increase reveals that given the actors remaining in the network, the dispersion of those collecting messages is not as great as when Elle and her takers are included. Be that as it may, a large discrepancy between the outdegree centralization index and the indegree index does persist, albeit to a lesser degree. The general pattern of a concentration of actors sending messages and a more diffuse group receiving them is still evident on the Forum even without the star actor.

Drawing a sociogram of the matrix excluding all ties to and from Elle (Figure 4.3) reveals why this pattern remains. There is no longer one central actor in the network, but there remains a clear core periphery structure to the network configuration. Indeed, a continuous core periphery model carried out excluding Elle retained a good fit between the model and the ideal pattern matrix, with a correlation coefficient of .846. Moreover, the model's recommended core

Figure 4.3. Sociogram of SOL-Cancer Forum binary message matrix—star actor excluded

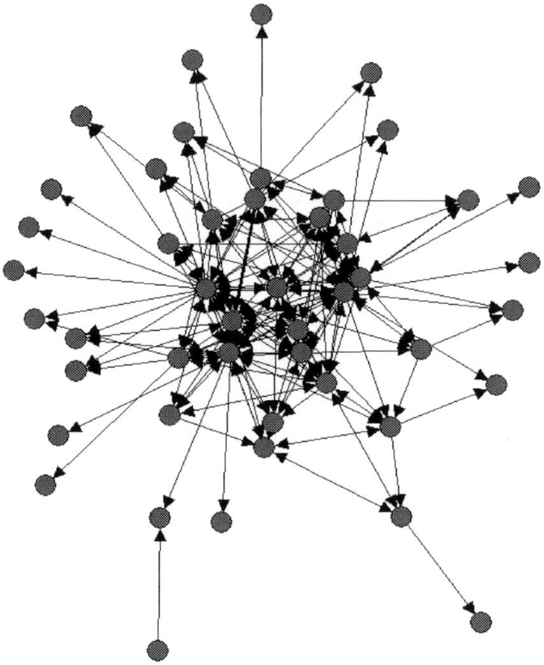

for this network is essentially the prime givers. Thus, it appears that Elle's unique contribution and dominant role is in single-handedly supporting most of the takers but not the other SOLers. Although Elle does send them a great number of support messages, the SOLers do not rely solely on her and provide one another with ample support messages. This is displayed in the sociogram in Figure 4.4, which retains the configuration of the original network, but with Elle and her ties removed. Many of the takers are no longer connected to the network, but the tight-knit cluster of SOLers remains.

Recalculating the actors' Freeman Degrees excluding the star actor further supports the notion of Elle's dominant role as the

Figure 4.4. Sociogram of SOL-Cancer Forum binary message matrix—star actor removed

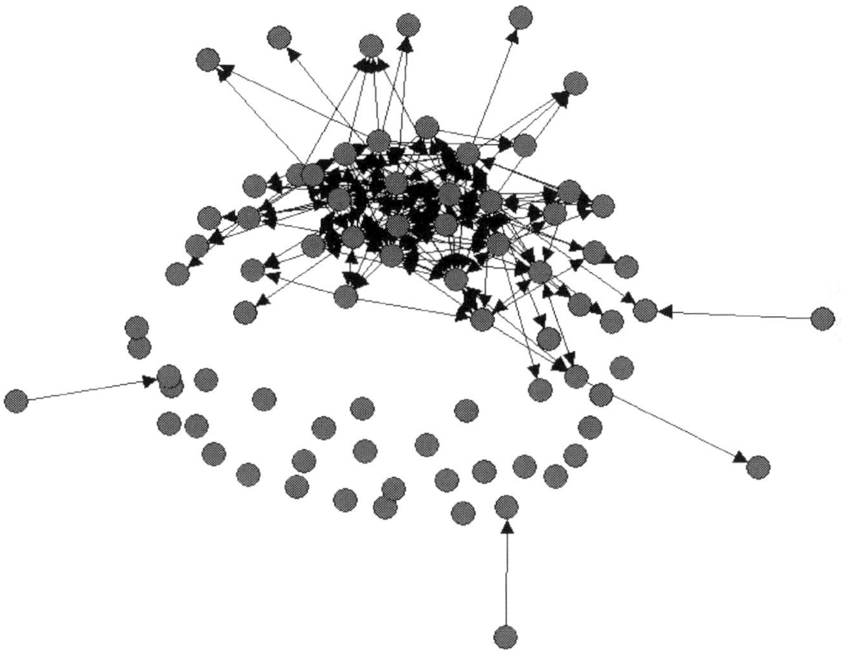

critical supporter of the takers but not the SOLers. Whereas none of the actors in any SOLer category are eliminated from the network when Elle is removed (Table 4.8), more than half the takers are (Table 4.9). Further, although the numbers of messages the SOLers send and receive are decreased, they remain substantial. Thus, these findings, along with all others analyzing the dominant role of the central actor, indicate the star outperforms all other actors in responding to first-time posters, nearly all of whom compose the takers. The takers section of the network would be most decisively affected by Elle's absence because she responds to 41 of the 48 takers and is the only actor who responds to 28 of them.

Table 4.8. Freeman Degree Centrality Measures—Valued and Binary Relations of Message Matrices—Excluding the Star Actor—SOLers

	Valued Freeman Degrees		Binary Freeman Degrees	
	Outdegree	Indegree	Outdegree	Indegree
		Cutpoint—prime givers		
Casey	99	64	27	19
Murray	57	48	20	16
Dee	48	38	23	14
Jenn	44	35	18	15
Nikki	36	30	14	11
Robin	25	35	14	15
		Cutpoint—serious members		
Breege	24	19	14	11
GwenQ	19	24	10	11
Joe	19	22	8	6
NikkiJ	16	14	7	7
Helen	16	11	10	4
Tessy	15	9	10	7
Chad	14	19	10	12
Stella	14	16	9	7
May	12	19	8	9
Dudley	10	14	7	8
		Cutpoint—moderate users		
Debby	9	10	5	4
PeggyH	9	9	6	6
Joicy	7	11	7	8
JoyAnn	6	6	5	4
Caroline	5	4	4	4
Betty	4	7	3	4
Nick	3	6	2	3
Brenda	3	4	3	3
Dawn	2	7	2	5
Charlotte	2	1	1	1
AnnF	1	4	1	3
Pa	1	2	1	2

(continued)

Table 4.8. *(continued)* Freeman Degree Centrality Measures—Valued and Binary Relations of Message Matrices—Excluding the Star Actor—SOLers

	Valued Freeman Degrees		Binary Freeman Degrees	
	Outdegree	Indegree	Outdegree	Indegree
Djmparrots	1	0	1	0
In4sports	1	0	1	0
Tammy	1	0	1	0
	Cutpoint—support takers			

Table 4.9. Freeman Degree Centrality Measures—Valued and Binary Relations of Message Matrices—Excluding the Star Actor—Takers

	Valued Freeman Degrees		Binary Freeman Degrees	
	Outdegree	Indegree	Outdegree	Indegree
Jennifer	0	5	0	4
Ron	0	3	0	3
Keming	0	3	0	3
Joan	0	2	0	2
JuneR	0	2	0	2
Maureen	0	2	0	2
StacyN	0	2	0	2
Pen	0	2	0	2
Jamie	0	2	0	2
CMD	0	2	0	1
CIGPIC	0	1	0	1
Lorella	0	1	0	1
Bob	0	1	0	1
Emily	0	1	0	1
MikeK	0	1	0	1
Ann	0	1	0	1
O'Kelly	0	1	0	1
MrsFarm	0	1	0	1
Ethel	0	1	0	1
Karen	0	1	0	1

On the other hand, although Elle does provide the SOLers with a very great number of support messages, the relations between them and the network they constitute would not fall apart without her. Casey's binary outdegree reveals that she contacts 27 of a possible 30 SOLers, demonstrating that she, along with the remaining five prime givers, would keep the SOLers' network running smoothly. All in all, were Elle to leave the Forum, another member would need to step into her role in supporting the takers or they would not get their needs met. On the other hand, the SOLers may need to increase their activity in supporting one another if they want to maintain the level of support messages they currently receive, but their supportive network would not disappear.

THE TRANSMISSION OF SOCIAL SUPPORT

The social structure of sending generally supportive messages between the five categories is now established, and the next step is to examine the patterns of transmitting specific types of support. It is important to keep in mind that when discussing the three kinds of support the unit of analysis is no longer a message but rather an instance of support. This is because of the fact that any message can contain more than one subcategory of each type of support. For example, a message conveying encouragement and understanding, both subcategories of emotional support, is coded as providing two instances of emotional support. First a collapsed matrix and then a density matrix of support transmitted within and between the categories are created for each kind of support (see Appendix B) to determine the behavior of the five groups in providing particular kinds of support. Comparing the findings from each of these methods demonstrates that the only essential variation between the social structures suggested by the two is the oscillating dominant role between the star and the prime givers. The two categories will be combined to reduce the complexity and highlight the larger social structures of the support networks because it has been established that the star stands out as the chief actor in relation to the takers but can be viewed as generally structurally equivalent with the prime givers in relation to the SOLers.

Density tables are created for all three kinds of support after collapsing the actors into the newly established four categories (Tables 4.10, 4.11, and 4.12). Included in the tables are the actual message counts of every cell. Each of these tables is transformed into a blockmodel represented by the three reduced sociograms (Figures 4.5, 4.6, and 4.7). In these sociograms, nodes that are darker in color have a density of self ties that are above the zeroblock threshold and those that are lighter in color do not. To create the blockmodels, the average density threshold was applied to both the emotional support matrix (0.918) and the companionship matrix (1.133). Applying the average density of 0.278 to the informational support network would have excluded both the moderate users and the takers. One half the average density (0.139) is employed instead, after considering that the densities of these cells are only slightly less than the average density, 0.210 and 0.238, respectively, and after considering the substantive knowledge of the star's far-reaching provision of informational support. All the densities designated zeroblocks in the emotional support matrix and the companionship matrix, however, are far removed from the density cutoffs, the smallest difference being 0.362.

Three general patterns in the transmission of specific kinds of support are displayed in these matrices and sociograms. First, in all three of these support networks only two categories of actors are responsible for providing significant amounts of support, the star plus prime givers and the serious members. The star plus prime givers consistently provide themselves with a significant quantity of all kinds of support and are solely responsible for providing the three other categories of actors with the various types of support each receives. The serious members reliably support the star plus prime givers with all kinds of support and supply themselves with salient amounts of emotional and informational support.

These findings point to another clearly visible structure, which is the durable relationship between the category containing the star plus prime givers and that of the serious members. There are consistently dense reciprocal ties between these two groups for all kinds of support throughout these matrices and sociograms. The matrices show that the first category provides the serious members with a bit more support of every kind, but the difference tends to be small and the serious members steadily provide the star plus prime givers with much more support than any other category. The actors in these groups share a multifaceted confidence that extends to every type of support transmitted on the Forum.

The third obvious pattern is the relationship between the number of categories of actors included in a support network and the amount of intimacy and interdependence associated with the corresponding kind of support. Informational support is a kind that can be requested of and provided to strangers. There is no need to be previously acquainted with a person to feel at ease communicating facts and passing on Web site addresses. The lack of intimacy involved in the transaction means there is very little personal investment required, and therefore providing informational support does not call for mutual support. Those categories that do not give much or anything at all still receive informational support in relevant amounts. As such, the informational support network is the largest, encompassing all four categories.

Emotional support, on the other hand, is not so easily exchanged with an unfamiliar person. It is a more intimate kind of support that requires a relationship with a greater amount of trust and interaction to be requested or provided. Actors need to dedicate time to cultivating such relationships. Accordingly, the one category excluded from this network, the takers, is made up of members who all post no more than one undirected message to the Forum. Conversely, the

Table 4.10. Emotional Support Density Matrix Including Message Counts—Four Categories

	Star plus prime givers	Serious members	Moderate users	Takers
Star plus prime givers	6.619 (278)	2.800 (196)	1.000 (105)	0.101 (34)
Serious members	2.343 (164)	0.989 (89)	0.140 (21)	0.023 (11)
Moderate users	0.495 (52)	0.120 (18)	0.038 (8)	0.013 (9)
Takers	0 (0)	0 (0)	0 (0)	0 (0)

Table 4.11. Informational Support Density Matrix Including Message Counts—Four Categories

	Star plus prime givers	Serious members	Moderate users	Takers
Star plus prime givers	1.667 (70)	1.100 (77)	0.210 (22)	0.238 (80)
Serious members	0.629 (44)	0.356 (32)	0.067 (10)	0.029 (14)
Moderate users	0.124 (13)	0.007 (1)	0.005 (1)	0.011 (8)
Takers	0 (0)	0 (0)	0 (0)	0 (0)

Table 4.12. Companionship Density Matrix Including Message Counts—Four Categories

	Star plus prime givers	Serious members	Moderate users	Takers
Star plus prime givers	10.500 (441)	3.100 (217)	0.771 (81)	0.057 (19)
Serious members	2.471 (173)	0.711 (64)	0.087 (13)	0.004 (2)
Moderate users	0.295 (31)	0.087 (13)	0.033 (7)	0.003 (2)
Takers	0 (0)	0 (0)	0 (0)	0 (0)

Figure 4.5. Reduced sociogram for emotional support blockmodel—four categories

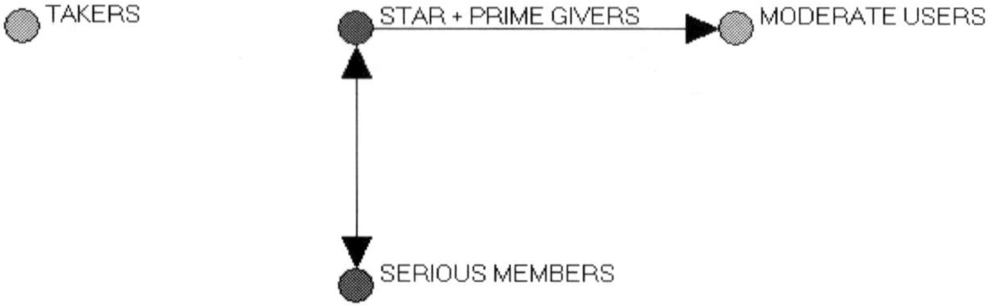

Figure 4.6. Reduced sociogram for informational support blockmodel—four categories

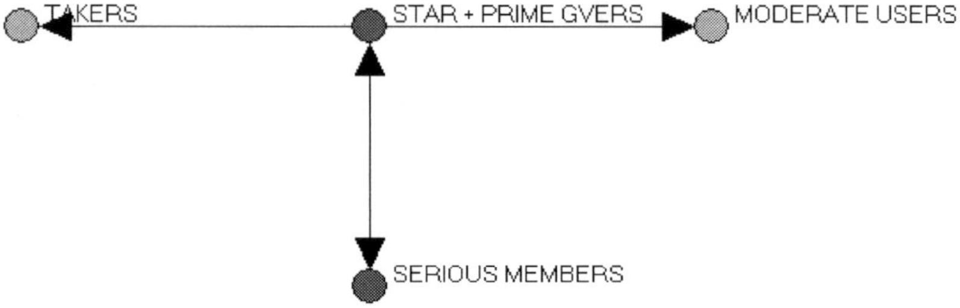

Figure 4.7. Reduced sociogram for companionship blockmodel—four categories

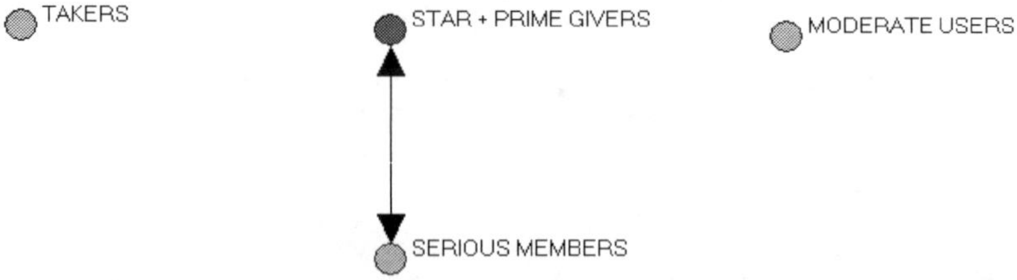

dominant category of the star plus the prime givers and the serious members share an intense relationship and exchange equally large amounts of emotional support. The moderate users, who have a more middling relationship with the other members of the Forum, are the sole category to receive a significant amount of emotional support without fully reciprocating. Nonetheless, they do send the dominant group 52 instances of emotional support, and even though this quantity is not large enough to be included in the blockmodel, it does amount to five times more than what the takers send.

Finally, the companionship network includes the smallest number of categories. Fittingly, this is the kind of support that requires the most confidence and reciprocity. It is described as message content that includes chatting and humor and, most importantly, does not focus on the subject of cancer. This type of support is exchanged among friends, those who have developed a sociable rapport that goes beyond the express purpose of the Forum. It requires the give-and-take that is inherent to friendly banter. The matrix reveals that for those included in the network it is the most dense support network. Predictably, the only two categories included in the companionship network are those that communally share all kinds of support.

Conclusion

The previous chapter described and analyzed the larger bifurcated structure of the SOL-Cancer Forum's electronic social network. The network was found to be divided between the givers, who transmitted support throughout the network, and the takers, who only received support without providing any. This chapter carries the analysis into the intricate and complex posting activity of the givers not explored in the previous chapter to provide a more detailed understanding of the Forum's social structure.

The givers uniformly identify as SOLers, but the contributions they make to the Forum vary greatly, creating a number of distinct positions and relations between them. A number of network procedures are conducted to identify these positions, the actors who occupy them, and their patterns of interaction. Initially a measure of actor level degree centrality results in the formation of four positional categories of SOLers. The star category contains one dominant actor who is the most prolific member in regard to sending and receiving messages. The second category is made up of six prime givers who send more messages than they receive and are second in posting behavior only to the star. The third group of serious members is composed of 10 actors who send and receive a fair number of messages, maintaining a steady presence on the Forum. Finally, the remaining 15 SOLers are categorized as the moderate users, who interact less frequently, but consistently, with other members of the Forum. A continuous core/periphery model confirms the star actor to be the central actor of the network, occupying a unique position. The findings also detail all other actors' positions in the network in relation to the star actor, substantiating the composition and characterization of the other three SOLer categories.

The network's social structure is then constructed based on the salient positions in the network, the specific actors who occupy those positions, and the patterns of interaction between them. The takers are now reintroduced into the analysis to establish the social structure of the entire network. A collapsed valued matrix reflecting the number of messages sent by the actors in each category is represented in a sociogram to provide the initial depiction of the ties between the five categories. The collapsed sociogram demonstrates the general give-and-take relationship among the SOLers but also reveals the inequitable nature of these exchanges. In addition, the star actor no longer occupies a central position in the network and appears to be surpassed by the prime givers in the number of messages sent. The creation of a surplus support matrix and sociogram demonstrates that the star is responsible for supporting the moderate users and the takers, who both predominantly collect support without reciprocating in kind. The prime givers provide the star with surplus support while she is supporting the moderate users and the takers. The serious members exchange an equitable amount of support with the Forum so that they are not indebted to anyone.

The question of the star actor's position of primacy is clarified by performing a number of network procedures using a matrix with all ties to and from the star actor removed. The findings reveal that the star occupies a unique position in relation to the takers, in that she is the sole actor who responds to more than half of them and is therefore their only connection to the network. Another actor would need to perform the role of the star actor in relation to the takers if she were to leave the network, or most of them would not be supported. The SOLers, on the other hand, are not predominantly reliant on the star for support. She does supply them with a great amount of support, but they amply support one another and thier network will not come apart without her.

The final analyses aim to uncover the way specific kinds of social support are transmitted in this social structure. Overall, the amount of reciprocal interaction actors engage in affects the depth and breadth of their relationships, which in turn determines the kinds of social support they exchange. Informational support is just as easily requested and provided by strangers as long-term friends because passing on factual information or a URL does not necessitate intimacy or dedication. On the other hand, the exchange of emotional support does involve personal cost like vulnerability and devotion. Actors who share this kind of support need to interact more often to develop intimate and trustworthy relationships. Companionship, which is made up of humor and content that do not focus on cancer, requires the greatest amount of confidence and reciprocity because actors need to have cultivated a friendly rapport that is sturdy enough to introduce humor to a cancer support group and is capable of moving beyond the express purpose of the Forum. Hence, the star, the prime givers, and the serious members are able to exchange all three kinds of support because of the vast number of messages they have exchanged, which have allowed them to cultivate the most durable, reciprocal, and profound relationships on the Forum. Not surprisingly, they are the only categories included in the companionship network, the most exclusive of the three. The moderate users interact with the other SOLers to a lesser extent but are still sufficiently engaged to establish the kind of trust and commitment that is required for emotional support. Conversely, the takers do not contribute anything to the Forum and therefore do not receive any support that requires a significant relationship. They are only part of the most inclusive network, receiving solely informational support.

These findings demonstrate how members' interactions in an electronic social network both construct the social structure of the group and influence the transmission of social support. Those who are most active have access to all kinds of support on account of the types of relationships such dedication leads to. On the other hand, actors who do not invest in a group cannot expect to get a lot out of it. The results also show the diversity in the kinds of support that can be found in an online forum. Actors in need of a wide range of supports need only dedicate the amount of time necessary to acquire the kind of support they are searching for. Equally, those who simply want a quick answer and are not able to make or interested in making a commitment can also get the support they desire.

Chapter 5

Designing a Network Support-Specific Model

In the preceding two chapters, network analytic procedures were applied to the data, resulting in a general understanding of the SOL-Cancer Forum's social structure and its influence on the transmission of three broad categories of social support. The next two chapters construct and employ a more refined theory and method to analyze the Forum's structure and understand its influence on the transmission of support. The current chapter develops the network support-specific model to analyze how online social support is transmitted within an electronic social network. To do so, first the expanded organizational contingency theory, which provides the theoretical foundation for this method, is delineated. This is followed by a description of the task-specific model upon which the network support-specific model is based. Finally, the design of the five dimensions that make up the network support-specific model is described. In the following chapter, hypotheses are generated based on the model, the dimensions of the model are operationalized, and hypotheses are tested.

Expanded Organizational Contingency Theory

To explain the relationship between social support and health, a number of theorists espouse either the buffer hypothesis or the direct effect hypothesis.[27] Litwak et al. (1989), however, view both these hypotheses as limited by first-order theoretical constructs. To overcome this limitation, the authors offer the expanded organizational contingency theory, a higher-level theoretical construct that provides a rationale as to why social support influences health and explains away both these hypotheses. The theory accomplishes this by introducing two conceptual distinctions into the study of social support and health that are lacking in other theoretical approaches. The first distinction stems from the basic premise that the structure of groups and the structure of tasks vary. For instance, groups can consist of a small number of people who excel at commonplace skills, such as a nuclear family, or a large number of people who are highly trained, such as a hospital's employees. Similarly, some tasks are better suited to a small number of people using everyday skills, whereas others tasks can be accomplished more efficiently by a large number of people using highly technical skills. Once the structures of groups and tasks are delineated, it is possible to discern which group can best perform which task by optimally matching their structures. For example, the health of a cancer patient who has severe fatigue after a chemotherapy session and no food at home would suffer if she did not eat or if she had to go food shopping. The task for which the patient needs assistance is not something an oncologist would perform but can easily be provided by a family member. Conversely, the provision of chemotherapy for this patient to fight her cancer is not a task a family member could provide, but rather doctors and nurses in an oncology unit.

The second conceptual distinction the theory introduces is the importance of distinguishing between health-related tasks that a group can and cannot provide. In the foregoing example, having the support of a primary group member for such a household task can have a positive effect on health, whereas relying on a doctor for such support will have a negative effect or no effect at all. On the other hand, turning to a primary group member for chemotherapy treatments would result in no change in health or an adverse one. Therefore, recognizing the health-related tasks that a group can and cannot perform makes it possible to explain the relationship between social support and health; that is, there will be a positive relationship between social support and health when a group is capable of performing a task that will ameliorate health and that group is present. Relying on a group to perform a task to enhance health when that group is not capable of performing such a task will produce a negative effect or none at all. In this way the expanded organizational contingency theory overcomes the limitations of the buffer and direct effect hypotheses by explaining that support from a group will produce a buffer effect when matched with a task that manages a crisis situation, and a main effect when matched with a task of a preventative nature.

In their work entitled "Organizational Theory, Social Support, and Mortality Rates: A Theoretical Convergence," Litwak et al. (1989) demonstrate how the expanded organization contingency theory illuminates the relationship between social support and health. The authors begin by theoretically articulating the relationship between tasks that can have an impact on specific causes of death and the group that can best perform such tasks. They explain that "[t]he expanded organizational contingency theory suggests that social support reduces mortality whenever available group resources match the type of service required to reduce a given cause of death" (Litwak et al. 1989, p. 54). To develop specific hypotheses reflecting this relationship, tasks are first differentiated on two dimensions, technical knowledge and everyday socialization, and then matched to the group that is more effective at accomplishing the tasks based on these two dimensions. For instance, informal groups will be more effective in performing tasks that require little technical knowledge and a high degree of knowledge gained through everyday socialization. The reasons for this are threefold: primary groups can perform such tasks for a lower cost with no expenditure on technical training; they are faster than formal organizations that move through hierarchical channels and codified rules; and they are more efficient being motivated by internalized commitment rather than economic incentive. After tasks are differentiated according to technical knowledge and everyday socialization, causes of death are also differentiated along these two dimensions according to whether group services that entail technical knowledge decrease the risk of death or services requiring everyday socialization decrease the risk of death (Litwak et al., 1989). The authors then display these relationships in Table 5.1, which they succinctly describe in the following paragraph:

> The rows of the table represent populations with the four possible combinations of high and low primary group and formal organizational resources. The columns distinguish causes of death according to whether group services, to reduce the risk of mortality, require either technical knowledge or everyday socialization or both. ... The numbers in the cells of the table represent the hypothesized ranking of causes-specific mortality for the four population groups (the rows) within each of the four causes-of-death categories (the columns)

Table 5.1. Hypothesized Rank of Mortality Rates by Formal and Informal Group Resources and Causes of Mortality (Classified by Services Needed to Reduce Them)

Group courses		causes of death (classified by technical knowledge and everyday socialization)			
Primary group	Formal org.	High socializ.[a]/low technical (Col. 1)	High socializ./high technical (Col. 2)	Low socializ./high technical (Col. 3)	Low socializ./low technical (Col. 4)
High	Low	1.00[b]	2.00	3.00	3.00
High	High	1.00	1.00	1.00	3.00
Low	High	3.00	2.00	1.00	3.00
Low	Low	3.00	3.00	3.00	3.00

Litwak, E., Messeri, P., Wolfe, S., Gorman, S., Silverstein, M., & Guilarte, M. (1989). Organizational theory, social support, and mortality rates: A theoretical convergence. *American Sociological Review, 54,* 53.

[a]High socializ./low technical causes are those in which the risk of death is reduced by services gained through everyday socialization and not requiring technical services.

[b]The numbers in the cells indicate the extent, if any, mortality rates will be reduced for row populations having designated group resources. A 1.00 corresponds to the population with the lowest hypothesized rate of mortality and a 3.00 means the highest mortality rate in each column.

> described above. Within any cause-of-death category (a column), the theory distinguishes at most three levels of mortality. The rank of "3" is used to designate, within each cause-of-death category, the group with the highest expected mortality. For instance, persons high in primary group support or resources but not formal organizational ones (row 1) will have a reduced risk of dying from causes prevented by services requiring only everyday socialization (e.g., pulling a cigarette out of the hands of a sleeping person) which are classified in column 1. Those in row 2, who are high on both formal and informal resources, will also have the primary group resources to reduce this cause of death. Therefore, the theory predicts that these two groups will have the lowest mortality rates, that is, a rank of 1 in rows 1 and 2 of column 1. Those in the lower two rows are low in primary group resources so they would have a higher mortality rate for this cause of death, that is, a rank of 3 in column 1 (Litwak et al., 1989, p. 53–54).

The authors provide the foregoing theoretical formulation and then go on to conduct an empirical test of the theory using the 1980 U.S. national mortality data. They begin with an empirical ranking of 176 causes of death in the International Classification of Disease, conducted by two health professionals[28] according to six group-service categories. The group-service categories are used to differentiate specific causes of death by the preventative effectiveness of group services on a six-point scale, with 1 representing the greatest effectiveness of formal influence and 6 that of primary groups. Married or single at time of death is used to measure primary group support. Mortality ratios are then calculated to establish the relationships between groups and causes of death. Their findings demonstrate that the effects of informal support on mortality vary according to the classification scheme put forth by their theory.

Hence, the expanded organization contingency theory exposes the shortcomings of both the buffer hypothesis and the direct effect hypothesis of social support. Informal social support will produce a main effect with nontechnical tasks of a preventative nature and a buffer effect for nontechnical crisis situations. Furthermore, in describing the interrelationship between the function of support and the structure of a group, this theory eliminates a salient problem in the field of social support research: the confounding of social support and social networks. Additionally, the theory demonstrates how and why social support affects health, providing a framework that can be applied to other instances of social support to predict which group can best provide support for which task.

A Task-Specific Model

A task-specific model of detailed optimal matching was developed to facilitate the application of the expanded organizational contingency theory to evaluating other kinds of support (Messeri et al., 1993). The expanded organizational contingency theory offers the theoretical premise that both groups and tasks can vary in structure, and the task-specific model provides a concrete classification of these structures. Two basic propositions provide the foundation for the theoretical framework of the expanded organizational contingency: The structure of groups varies, for example: the structure of a primary group compared with a formal organization, and the structure of tasks that provide support vary, for instance, the variation between giving friendly advice and giving a medical diagnosis. The task-specific model builds on these foundations to provide a systematic method by which varying group and task structures can be matched. To that end, the model details seven structural dimensions that simultaneously vary for both groups and tasks: proximity, length of commitment, commonality of lifestyle, size, type of motivation, division of labor, and level of technical knowledge (Table 5.2). The first four dimensions of the model are fashioned to

Table 5.2. Structural Dimensions for Matching Group Properties to Task Characteristics

Dimensions	Group characteristics	Task characteristics
Proximity	Continuous proximity	Coordination requires continuous, face-to-face contact
	Distant, ad hoc proximity	Coordination or interaction can be conducted either at a remote distance or for short periods of time
Length of commitment	Long-term commitment	Expenditure of substantial time or resources required
	Limited commitment	Minimal expenditure of time or effort; different individuals can substitute in performing tasks over time
Commonality of lifestyle or major social role	Common lifestyle	Task performance benefits from shared experience, e.g., common roles
	Dissimilar lifestyle	Skills or attributes not common among occupants of common roles, e.g., age, employment, gender, ethnicity
Size	Small size	Task not easily subdivided among several people
	Large size	Task can be divided among many people or interchangeably performed by many persons
Sources of motivations	Economic incentive	Easily observed, tasks requiring extended time and effort
	Internalized motivation	Highly contingent, difficult to monitor
Division of labor	Detailed division of labor	Standardized or ability to divide services
	Nonspecific division of labor	Unpredictable or subject to many contingencies

(continued)

Table 5.2. *(continued)* Structural Dimensions for Matching Group Properties to Task Characteristics

Dimensions	Group characteristics	Task characteristics
Level of technical knowledge	High-level recruitment based on merit and technical expertise	Technically complex, e.g., requires specialized training
	Low-level recruitment based on ascriptive ties, not merit	Simple, learned through everyday socialization

Messeri, P., Silverstein, M., & Litwak, E. (1993). Choosing optimal support groups: A review and reformulation. *Journal of Health and Social Behavior, 34,* 125.

capture the salient structural features of groups and tasks. The final three dimensions are included specifically to differentiate between tasks best suited to the primary group versus a formal organization.

For example, in regard to the dimension of proximity, a group is identified as having close continuous contact or distant ad hoc contact, and a task is identified as benefiting from close continuous contact or distant ad hoc contact. Then a group that requires close continuous contact is matched to a task that benefits from close continuous contact, establishing that group as capable of providing the specific support entailed in the task. For example, the marital dyad has close continuous contact, whereas kin tend to have more distant ad hoc contact. Nightly meals are prepared mostly in the home on a continuous basis as opposed to celebratory meals, which can be held in a distant location on an ad hoc basis. Matching groups and tasks along the dimension of proximity reveals the marital dyad as best suited to providing nightly meals, whereas kin are better suited to providing celebratory meals.

The authors assert that the expanded organizational contingency theory provides a framework that can be modified to focus on different groups and/or tasks according to the nature of social support in specific groups. To that end, the task-specific model will be adapted and applied to the study of social support in an online forum to identify when and how social support is provided. To do so, the focus on group structure must be reoriented and the dimensions of the task-specific model amended to suit the distinctive environment of online relations. These processes culminate in the development of the network support-specific model, which will be used to analyze relations and support on the SOL-Cancer Forum. The dimensions of the network support-specific model along with the corresponding dimensions of the task-specific model that inspired them are presented in Table 5.3, and Table 5.2 details the original task-specific model.

A NETWORK SUPPORT-SPECIFIC MODEL

It is first necessary to shift from analyzing group properties to studying network properties or, more precisely, electronic network properties to apply the framework of optimal matching to the online Forum. The characteristics of relations contained in the Forum are much too varied and novel to be accurately represented by a common form of group, for example, friends or neighbors, or classified by any definition of a single group at all. Making a priori assumptions about the relations between members forfeits the ability to distinguish and analyze meaningful group relations from the larger collectivity that is simply a group in name. A social network perspective, however, allows the characteristics and patterns of relations to emerge from the Forum rather than being imposed by external categories. Viewing the Forum as an electronic social network provides the opportunity to distinguish and categorize meaningful patterns of relations from the larger collectivity and then analyze their relationships with the transmission of social support.

Table 5.3. Structural Dimensions for Matching Electronic Social Network Characteristics With Online Support Characteristics[29]

Dimension	Electronic social network characteristics	Online support characteristic	Corresponding group characteristic
Level of dedication	Frequent contact	Necessitates continuous monitoring and frequent interaction	Proximity
	Sporadic contact	Necessitates little monitoring and interaction	
Degree of intimacy	Strong ties made up of recurrent contact	Requires personal devotion and confidence; benefits from an established rapport	Source of motivation, level of technical knowledge
	Weak ties made up of ad hoc contact	Requires no personal devotion or confidence; benefits from access to novel information	
Reciprocity	Symmetrical relations	Demands abiding personal investment and commitment	Length of commitment
	Asymmetrical relations	Demands little personal investment and commitment	
Size	Small	Suited to a small number of actors	Size
	Large	Suited to a large number of actors	
Commonality of major cancer role	Homogeneous ties based on common role in relationship to cancer	Benefits from sharing a similar experience and perspective	Commonality of major social role
	Heterogeneous ties based on dissimilar role in relationship to cancer	Benefits from exposure to an opposing experience and perspective	

As such, characterizing all those who participate in an online forum as one group would not only be substantively inaccurate but also analytically limiting.

Viewing the SOL-Cancer Forum as an electronic social network rather than a group makes it possible to amend the task-specific model to reflect the structural dimensions along which the Forum's network and support will be evaluated for optimal matching. The network support-specific model was influenced by three sources: the dimensions of the task-specific model (Table 5.3); the traditional social support and social network literatures; and features of the SOL-Cancer network that reflect distinct patterns of online behavior and supportive interactions. All five of the network support specific-model's dimensions are based on network characteristics that reflect actors' positions in the online network.

The network support-specific model also differs from the task-specific model in that the new model problematizes requests for support and treats them as distinct tasks. Traditional social support theory assumes that requests and provisions of support are bound together, that is, an individual receives support from the person he or she requested it of. However, online forums empirically allow requests and provisions to be decoupled because all actors receive each request for support and it is acceptable for anyone to respond, regardless of who the request was directed to. In fact, in many cases the person to whom a request was directed is not the only person to respond. In that way, the support transmitted in an online forum permits requests to be viewed as distinct tasks that can be scrutinized to determine what, if any, structural constraints are placed on the act of requesting support in an electronic social network. Such structural constraints may also be more relevant in online forums because requests are commonly broadcast to all members. An online broadcast is sent to roughly 84 members, unlike face-to-face support groups, where a request may be voiced to 10 members seated around a group. These exceptional features of online requests allow the network support-specific model to be applied to requests for support to predict how they may be governed by the principles of expanded organizational contingency theory.

Model Dimensions

Level of Dedication

The first dimension of the network support-specific model is level of dedication. This dimension assesses each member's level of dedication to the SOL-Cancer Forum by the amount of contact the individual makes with the Forum. Those who are highly dedicated to the group respond to messages or post new threads on a continuous, at times daily, basis. In contrast, posters with little or no dedication participate sporadically or even just once. Correspondingly, some kinds of support necessitate continuous monitoring and frequent interaction with the Forum to be accomplished, whereas others can be fulfilled with little monitoring and interaction. An individual who does not continuously follow others' postings is not likely to become interested in or even knowledgeable about current situations and, therefore, is not going to provide attentive caring and concern. On the other hand, posting a one-off request for basic information about thalidomide without previously having participated in the Forum is commonplace.

The dimension of proximity from the original model inspired the dimension level of dedication. Proximity identifies groups as having either continuous close proximity or distant ad hoc proximity. Tasks are classified according to whether coordination requires continuous face-to-face contact or can be conducted infrequently or from a distance. Groups and tasks are then matched for optimal support. Here is an example:

> continuous face-to-face contact is [necessary] in helping disabled persons bathe, dress, and eat. In contrast, modern technology permits caregivers to provide advice or verbal emotional support, financial aid, or household help in dealing with acute illness, through telephone calls, fax machine messages, or ad hoc visits by airplane or automobile (Messeri et al., 1993, p. 124).

The SOL-Cancer Forum does not contain any face-to-face interaction, so support for tasks that require tangible assistance is not possible. Nonetheless, research conducted on traditional social networks demonstrates that although not being in physical close contact does negatively influence instrumental social support, other types of support are not negatively affected by contemporary means of transportation and communication. Wellman and Wortley (1990) report that "physical access promotes small and large services.... [h]owever, physical access is not related to other dimensions of support because people are able to provide some forms of companionship, emotional aid, and financial aid over long distances" (p. 569). Moreover, the dimension of proximity not only represents face-to-face contact but is also a measure of continuous contact to provide support for tasks that require it. Members who are dedicated to the Forum can provide continual support for assistance with emotional, informational, and companionship needs by consistently monitoring the list and interacting with those in need as their requests are posted. For example, Dudley, a new member, quickly follows his initial post for information with an emotional e-mail about his new diagnosis and growing fear. He explains:

> ... I'm trying to find out all I can because I have it and it spread to my lymph nodes in dec. when it was diagnosed and now tomorrow I find out the results if it has spread more. I'm real scared and this has helped. What do I do on this forum? I need help.

This post, along with every one of his nearly daily messages over the next five days are met with anywhere from two to five responses from dedicated members monitoring his progress to help him through the fear and anxiety he naturally feels as his journey with cancer begins. Breege, who has posted nearly every day since she joined the group in the beginning of the month, replies with understanding, empathy, and encouragement:

> Welcome Dudley, I'm also new to this forum yet feel as if I'm talking and hearing from good friends... Like you, I'm also waiting on test results to see how my future is to be determined. You will be in my prayers and hope you will remember me in yours. ...

Indeed, the provision of frequent continual support is facilitated within online forums because members can access them from home or work at any time they need to or is convenient for them. Having easy access to an online support forum at any time of the day makes the maintenance of continuous contact possible and practical.

In regard to specific types of support, members who post and reply on a continuous basis also tend to develop more profound relationships that enable them to share a variety of supports. Those with a high level of dedication eventually begin to share emotional support and companionship that goes beyond the rubric of cancer support. Their posts and replies read more like a long-distance asynchronous conversation than e-mail posts to a cancer forum. The thread below demonstrates part of one day's online interaction between highly dedicated members providing companionship in sharing the experience of a snowy Sunday:

> It snowed here in New York all day yesterday. I awoke to a winter wonderland. The sun glistening off the snow and seeing the landscape and trees all covered in a beautiful blanket of fluffy white is indeed awesome! Now to clear

> a path in the walkway so that we can all go to grandma's and celebrate the 8th birthday of my twins, Brianna and Caitlin.
>
> All the kids are looking forward to sledding down the hill of the park across the road from us. There is a certain peace that descends along with the snow… another gift from God.
> Joe
>
> You know Joe, I watched an old movie to get into the spirit of the snowfall last night: "Yes, Virginia, there is a Santa Claus." It was set in 1890s New York. Anyway, I was impressed just realizing how nice (and how different) a snowfall was then. You didn't hear the rumble of snowblowers and plows, but the soft tinkle of bells on horses. The snow didn't turn black from exhaust in a day or two (yellow and brown maybe?) and the softer sounds of those days must have been such a joy! But then maybe our modern noisy world makes us even more appreciative and more aware of those wonderful, almost holy, "silent nights."–robin
>
> So very true my friend. As for the white snow… just remember that in those days there was a lot more soot due to fossil burning fuel… a lot of fire places to keep warm and a lot of horse stuff left on the street! …
> Joe

Degree of Intimacy

The next dimension, degree of intimacy, is a measure of the strength of the relationship between two members on the Forum and the kind of information that relationship offers access to. In tradition social network research, when Granovetter (1973) introduced the concept of tie strength, he described it as "a combination of time, the emotional intensity, the intimacy, and reciprocal services which characterize the tie" (p. 1361) (for discussion, see Marsden & Campbell, 1984). At the same time, his theory of the strength of weak ties placed their importance in bridging those who are not directly tied and transmitting unique information not available from strong ties (Granovetter, 1973; see also Liu & Duff, 1972). On those grounds, tie strength is used here to indicate the intimacy of a tie and its access to unique information. Any two members who send each other messages in this electronic social network often create strong ties with one another and develop a great amount of intimacy. Such relationships are characterized by the easy flow and deep caring evident in the endearing terms and nicknames they use for one another, their depth of knowledge of each other's lives, and the very personal experiences they share with one another. Conversely, other dyads may never even complete one mutual exchange, have very weak ties with little or no intimacy, and, in some cases, may not even give their names. These relationships, although lacking in depth, prove to be very useful for the exchange of basic information, which does not require intimacy to be freely requested and provided.

There are some types of social support that require personal devotion and confidence, as well as an established familiarity, whereas others require no personal devotion and confidence but benefit from access to novel information. To demonstrate, members with strong ties who have developed a high degree of intimacy can bring humor into the relationship even when discussing cancer and tease each other about feeling sorry for oneself. In contrast, those pairs made up of weak ties are not likely to share the degree of intimacy that would allow such lightheartedness and are better suited to requesting and providing information about a certain type of cancer.

The creation of this dimension was influenced by two dimensions of the task-specific model: source of motivation and level of technical knowledge. Source of motivation is included in the original model to differentiate primary groups from formal organizations according to whether members' motivation is based on internalized affection or economic incentive. Tasks are categorized as requiring internalized affection if they are difficult to monitor, or as requiring economic incentive if they demand extended time and effort (Messeri et al., 1993). To illustrate the matching of characteristics of groups and tasks along this dimension, if you get stuck working Saturday morning, someone in your home is best suited to wash your good luck shirt for the big game that afternoon; however, to wash the entire team's uniforms after the game, a laundry service would be best suited. The dimension of source of motivation corresponds to degree of intimacy insofar as those who share strong ties tend to be motivated by a mutual sense of devotion and dependence shared by those in an intimate relationship. Conversely, members with weak ties are more commonly motivated by more self-serving motivations such as making their contribution to the more general work of the Forum or personally acquiring knowledge or assistance. Likewise, a supportive task can be classified as very demanding, hence requiring personal devotion or not very involved and thus satisfied by more superficial self-interested motives. To demonstrate, Nikki and Kelly have formed an intimate bond on the SOL-Cancer Forum and both refer to Nikki as Kelly's mom. Kelly, however, has recently been very busy and has not posted much on the SOL-Cancer Forum. Kelly's eventual post brings the "biggest smile" to Nikki's face, and she swiftly writes:

> Hi Kel, Where have you been. I lost your address when my PC crashed, now I have a different server. I am so happy to get your address again. Now you can write back to your Sol Mom. Let me know how it goes with you. Did you hear PJ had her Baby and it was a girl, in Jan.? Love ya, Mom (Nikki)

In Kelly's response we see that although she has not written to Nikki, she has still been concerned with Nikki's tribulations and has kept up with her posts:

> Dear Mom, I am so glad that PJ had a perfect baby. They must be so overjoyed. I have been following your trials with Paul and saying my prayers for you both—all—including your mom. Life has been very busy. ... My younger son, Robby, is first dealing with my cancer and not well. We are busy trying to get him on track. ... Please send me your snail mail address as I have something I want to send you. It was so good to hear from you, lets not loose touch again. Love, :-) Kelly

Nikki and Kelly do maintain their correspondence, and, even though Kelly only has time to write one message each to three other members during the sample period, she and Nikki manage to exchange messages on seven out of the remaining eleven days.

In contrast, members who have weak ties that are lacking in intimacy tend to be motivated by more self-serving interests. For example, a one-time poster sends the following message to the list and simply signs it with his e-mail address: "Sir Would you happen to know which company owns drug cgp57148b? Thank you cobb@earthlink.net." Jenn's response is short and to the point, simply doing the job of providing cobb with the information he requests: "This has been renamed to STI-571 and I believe it is made by Novartis toll free line is 1 800 340 6843. Jenn."

Level of technical knowledge is the second dimension of the task-specific model that is reflected in the new dimension of degree of intimacy. As stated previously, the strength of a tie has been found to be associated with the kind of information that passes through it (Granovetter, 1973). In the original model, level of technical knowledge differentiates primary groups from formal organizations by revealing recruitment as based on merit and technical expertise or ascriptive ties. Tasks are then sorted according to the level of technical complexity they require based on specialized training or skills learned through common socialization (Messeri et al., 1993). Groups and tasks are matched along this dimension such that a hospital would provide the best treatment for pneumonia, but mom's tender loving care and chicken soup would provide the best care for a cold. This is reflected in the dimension of degree of intimacy in that, although SOL-Cancer members are not recruited based on technical expertise or ascriptive ties, individuals who choose to have recurrent contact with other members and those who only have ad hoc contact tend to be distinguished by level of specialized knowledge. This is characterized as a high level of lay expertise regarding the experience of cancer or as a novice, lacking in basic specialized knowledge. An actor's level of knowledge is distinguished by her proficiency or ignorance in the fundamentals regarding the cancer afflicting her life. It is revealed by an in-depth, intricate question or very basic, straightforward question. For example, a common beginner's question is:

> My father was recently diagnosed with neuroendocrine cancer. What is the treatment for this? Is this the same thing as poorly differentiated neuroendocrine carcinomas?

In contrast Dee, who makes frequent contact with a number of members, posts a question that moves beyond the basics and delves deeper into the cancer experience:

> Hi Elle, I have a quick question. You said you had some info on how to talk to kids about cancer, can you post something. As this has progressed, I would like to know what the "experts" say about talking to small children about this. So far, I have just told Chance that NaNa has poison in her stomach and that the Dr.'s are trying to get it out. Thanks Elle, Dee

Regarding social support, this example also demonstrates the difference in the type of informational support that is provided and requested through ties that have different degrees of intimacy. Granovetter (1973) demonstrated the advantage of weak ties in traditional social networks to be in the access they offer to novel information. "...[T]hose to whom we are weakly tied are more likely to move in circles different from our own and will thus have access to information different from that we receive" (p. 1371) (see also Liu & Duff, 1972). In this kind of electronic social network, which focuses on a particular illness, there is a collection of lay experts that can easily be accessed by those who need information about the disease without having to establish an intimate relationship so that weak ties can provide novel information. In addition, information can further be distinguished as basic or complex, with weak ties tending to request and provide fundamental facts and strong ones exchanging more intricate knowledge.

Reciprocity

Reciprocity is a dimension that evaluates the symmetry of message sending between actors. Some members sustain a balanced exchange of messages by consistently responding to each other. Actors need to be committed to one another and willing to invest a significant amount of time and attention to their relationship to maintain this kind of communication. Conversely, other members send a rare reply or none at all, resulting in conversations that are lopsided or nonexistent. Failing to respond to someone who has taken the time to write you displays a lack of interest or obligation. Similarly, certain kinds of support require the kind of intimacy and reliance found in a relationship that entails a large personal investment and deep commitment. Such relationships make actors feel safe sharing painful experiences or depending on someone for encouragement when times are tough. On the other hand, there are types of support that do not demand confidence or loyalty and can easily be accomplished without reciprocity. For example, requesting factual information about a type of cancer treatment or a reliable Web site.

Length of commitment is the dimension from the original model that corresponds to reciprocity. It is defined by three criteria: the expenditure of time to perform a service; the expenditure of resources to perform a service; and whether the same individual is needed to perform a service over time. These criteria are used to differentiate groups with members who have long-term commitments from those that have limited commitments, as well as tasks that require a large or small amount of time or resources. Based on these criteria, groups and tasks can matched as follows:

> For instance, in order to provide daily household services, such as preparation of food or the provision of help with personal grooming, i.e., dressing and shaving, long-term commitment is required. By contrast, minimal commitment is required for a neighbor to call the fire department when noticing a house on fire (Messeri et al., 1993, p. 124).

Online forums are not capable of providing instrumental tasks such as these, yet the underlying principles of the two dimensions are similar. The maintenance of a reciprocal relationship or lack of it depends on the expenditure of time and amount of devotion much like the instrumental tasks described in the foregoing. For example, Elle and Joe have a long-standing persistent pattern of mutual message exchange. Whenever one of them posts a message to the other, a quick response is assured. Actors must spend time reading posts and faithfully returning to the Forum to facilitate this kind of give-and-take. Elle and Joe have cultivated such a close relationship that they refer to one another as auntie and nephew. Moreover, this profound relationship allows them to exchange messages that contain both sober concern and lighthearted joking. Elle is a two-time cancer survivor, and during the sample period her husband, Robert, receives a diagnosis of prostate cancer. She has just informed the SOLers that she is a new grandmother, and she and Joe share the following exchange of messages:

> Ah my dear Auntie/Grandma! What great news. I am sure that this is one time you don't mind being worn out!! Also happy to hear that Robert is taking a more pro-active role in his treatment… that moment was certainly a defining one in my journey. Tell him it is now time to be the kicker instead of the kickie!! Give that bundle of joy a big hug and kiss for me… no, not Robert! God Bless and I love you. Joe

> Just gave Robert that kiss for you, ooops! You meant the baby. No wonder he looked at me funny. He can be the kickie all he wants, my pleasure (don't you take that the wrong way you naughty boy!). Ah, defining moments, I am sure you well remember mine and I was a year late! But we are all still here plugging and fighting… . Amen to survivors! Tough old cookies huh? Love, Aunti El

Conversely, actors who do not invest their time and attention do not developing intimate and mutually supportive relationships and tend to mostly send or receive formal messages containing factual information. For example, Ron's first post to the Forum is simply a very direct question, "Does anyone know if Adenocarcinoma can be a primary cancer in the liver? GI tract is negative. Ron" Jenn replies with the information he is requesting, but since they have no established relationship and Ron's message does not convey any interest in forming or fostering one, her message is not one that requires a great investment of time or sentiment:

> If this works properly, you should be able to click on the embedded links. Adenocarcinom is a subset of the all inclusive term carcinoma. Did not find anything on a primary adenocarcinoma in the liver. http://www.graylab.ac.uk/cgibin/omd?adenocarcinoma

Size

The next dimension of size characterizes a message as small or large according to whether it is sent to a small or large size group of actors. Messages sent to a small size group are addressed and directed to specific members, and those sent to a large size group are broadcast to the entire Forum. A message directed to small size groups indicates that such support is better suited to a small number of actors, whereas a message broadcast to the Forum is for the kind of support better suited to a large set of actors. Different types of support are more suitable to diverse size groups according to whether support benefits from access to a small select group who are highly dedicated and specialized or from access to a large pool of others with a wider range of knowledge and resources.

The task-specific model also contains the dimension of size where it is employed to classify a group as small or large and a task as easily subdivided among several people or not. The authors provide the following example to illustrate the dimension:

> For instance, helping someone get dressed may be done faster by one person than by ten, but having a large number of helpers is beneficial for spotting burglary attempts when residents are away and for dealing with cash flow problems (Messeri et al., 1993, p. 125).

This is similar to the network support-specific model's dimensions of size, with the exclusion of tasks that require physical contact. A member of the SOL-Cancer Forum who is searching for useful basic information on a type of cancer will be better off posting a broadcast message that is not directed to any particular individual and therefore intended for everyone. In this manner the message will most likely be read by a great number of actors, increasing the likelihood that a member who is knowledgeable on the subject will read the post and the sender will receive the information he or she seeks, most often rather quickly. For example, Josephine broadcasts the following request to the entire Forum:

> I have just found out that my father has Adeno Carcinoma on his right side of his prostate. Please help me

> find some information on this matter. Is this just a name for Prostate Cancer. His Gleason level is A 7. This information comes from a biopsy on his prostate. Please send all the websites and information you can. Thanks for all your help. Josephine Taylor

Within a few hours Elle has posted the following reply:

> Hi Josephine: Yes, it is prostate cancer, adenocarcinoma, mean's cancer of a organ. His Gleason is a bit high; so he must have had it for a while, prostate cancer is usually slow growing; but he will need to watch that it dose not matesize. My husband just had sterotatic radiosurgy for this with the seed implants first and this is a non invasive treatment. In order words when men have surgery they quite often have urinary problems and erectal dysfunction. With the seed implants and radiosurgery very few have this problem. This certainly helps on the emotional aspect. Infact, with-in a day most men are back to work. The only difficulties my husband had was constipation. Hope this has helped you and if we may be of further help, please don't hesitate to ask.Warmly, Elle

In contrast, an actor who is looking for sympathy, a type of support that is more demanding, benefits from sending a directed message to one of the highly dedicated SOLers who is acquainted with the requester's experience and feelings. To illustrate, after Dee sends an message asking if "anyone else need[s] [the pity pot] for a while" now that she is done with it, Breege sends a message to Dee expressing her need for it since she is feeling very down:

> Yes, Dee... I'd like to borrow the pity pot for awhile if it's free..it's been 2 years now since I lost my best friend to cancer (she was 44,newly married and happier than she had been in years.) Her cancer was extremely aggressive and took her from us without even time to say good-bye. Only 2 weeks before I had lost my beloved father but God was kind and gave us time to tell him all those things you forget to say in everyday life. (I no longer forget or

> assume there will be time "later")… I will try not to sink too low but it would be good to have a "pot" to catch me in case I do…

Dee quickly responds with the sympathy Breege is requesting.

Commonality of Major Cancer Role

The last dimension of the network support-specific model is commonality of major cancer role. Members on the Forum occupy a variety of roles in relationship to cancer including cancer patient and caregiver, as well as adult child, more distant relative, and friend of a cancer patient. This dimension categorizes members according to these roles since the experience of occupying each of them differs from the others. Support can benefit from sharing with those who have had a similar experience or from exposure to those who have an alternative perspective. Other patients can provide a great amount of empathy for those who are newly diagnosed with a unique understanding of being the one who has cancer in a way that members in any other role cannot. On the other hand, those who have a family member with cancer would be best to offer support when a patient wants to know firsthand how her family feels about her diagnosis.

Commonality of major cancer role in the network support-specific model corresponds to commonality of lifestyle in the initial model where it is used to differentiate groups whose members share a common lifestyle from those with a dissimilar lifestyle. Tasks are classified as benefiting from "shared experiences" or from "skills and attributes" that are not held in common. Groups and tasks are then matched for support as in the following example:

> [R]ecent retirees learning how to adapt to their new way of life are likely to obtain the best advice from retired friends or acquaintances who share similar lifestyles.

> ...[whereas a] disabled older person in need of assistance with bathing or moving about .... require[s] help from persons who are physically strong (i.e., younger). In this situation, their adult children are likely to be better sources of support than their age-peer friends (Messeri et al., 1993, p. 124).

The online Forum cannot offer physically assistance of the kind detailed in this example, yet the foundational concept that certain kinds of support benefit from sharing a similar experience and role, whereas others do not, is reflected in the new dimension. The importance of experiential similarity in providing support is reinforced by Suitor, Pillemer, and Keeton's (1995) study of the support that both family caregivers and returning students receive from their social networks. The authors set out to "determine whether the [positive supportive] effects of homophily occur because social statuses play such a dominant role in structuring individuals' identities, or because people who occupy similar positions within the social structure are also likely to share life experiences" (p. 1575). Their findings demonstrate that for both groups the important aspect of homophily in regard to whether or not network members provided support was indeed experiential similarity. This relationship was found at the initial time of transition and one year later (p. 1580). An example of this can be seen in the SOL-Cancer Forum when Dudley, a newly diagnosed cancer patient, posts to the Forum requesting information on melanoma:

> ...I'm trying to find out all I can because I have it and it spread to my lymph nodes in dec. when it was diagnosed and now tomorrow I find out the results if it has spread more. I'm real scared and this has helped. ...

Casey, another patient whose cancer is in remission, attempts to soothe Andy's fear by providing the kind of encouragement that is most reassuring when coming from someone who has been there and made it through. She also shares her own fears and firsthand advice on what helped her endure:

> Dear Dudley: I have to go tomorrow, too—for my two year checkup. I was diagnosed with small cell lung cancer in December of 1997—declared "clean" in March of 1998. I know exactly what you're going through—trust me! My prognosis was very bad—25%—and I was scared to death. The chemo was very aggressive and made me very sick. However, my doctor was extremely compassionate, and gave me everything I needed to make it more bearable. Ask for Zophran for the nausea, if Procompazine doesn't work. I took Xanax and Ativan for the anxiety, morphine for the pain, Ambien to sleep at night. Needless to say, I was a zombie a good part of the time, but it was better than the alternative. I remember so clearly how awful it was, but I'm well today. Hang in there, friend. Your friend—Casey

Dudley's next message reveals the results of his test and reports that he will be in a clinical trial. He expresses that he is "going crazy but it is nice to know people have gotten thru it." Casey continues her empathic and encouraging peer support:

> Dear Dudley: I'm so glad you've been accepted into a clinical trial. This is really wonderful news. As you know, I was in a clinical trial myself. I know I wouldn't be here today if I hadn't been. You're going to be fine, my friend. Casey

The following example demonstrates the benefits of interacting with those who occupy different roles. Lucia, a member whose mother has not been given very long to live, writes to the Forum explaining her mother's situation:

> My Mom is the one with cancer it started in the lung and went to the brain and the pancreas, and the bones.

> They say there is no cure and all they can do is radiate the whole brain to keep it from growing and hopefully shrink the tumor in her stomach so that she can eat. She is on pain meds to help releave some of the paon from the pncreas and the back. They say hopefully it will buy us a year but there is no hope of a cure. Thanks for the support as I will be needing it. Love and Light Lucia

Breege, a patient who was also told there was no cure, is capable of providing Lucia with some hope by recounting her own experience:

> Hi Lucia. I'm so sorry to hear of your mom's suffering but remember that there is a world of difference between "no cure" and "no hope." Many of us, myself included, were given little chance of survival yet are still here. The main thing I have learned, through all of this, is to view each day as the gift it is and not focus on what tomorrow may (or may not) bring. Try to be thankful for every minute you have together. …

Furthermore, since Breege suffers from a great amount of pain associated with her cancer like Lucia's mother, she is also in a position to address this aspect of Lucia's concern for her mom by providing advice and encouragement:

> I don't know your mom but I suffer a lot of pain as well and there is nothing that breaks thru my pain so effectively as a good laugh… humor is often the best gift you can give. Be strong, Lucia but don't be afraid to be weak sometimes, too. We'll be here for you whenever you need us and your family will be included in my prayers. Your friend, Breege

Conclusion

These five dimensions make up the network support-specific model that can be used to classify structural features of both an electronic network and online support so that they may be optimally matched. The following chapter presents the application of this model to the SOL-Cancer Forum to uncover how and when social support is transmitted within this electronic social network. To do so, hypotheses are formulated for each category of support, the five dimensions are then operationalized, and, finally, hypotheses are evaluated in light of the model's findings.

Chapter 6

Applying a Network Support-Specific Model

An electronic social network creates ties that allow the exchange of resources among network members as in a traditional social network; however, there are differences between the two (Costigan, 1999; Fernbach, 1999; Garton, Haythornthwaite, & Wellman, 1999). The most obvious aspect of these differences is the lack of physical contact and interactions. Moreover, research on traditional networks demonstrates that different networks provide different kinds of support and individuals do not receive all kinds of support from any one tie (Wellman & Gulia, 1999). Hence with the network support-specific model fully developed, the research task is to evaluate whether the structure of the Forum's electronic social network matches the structure of online social support, thus making it possible to determine when and how social support is transmitted on the SOL-Cancer Forum.

To that end, hypotheses are developed that predict the structural features of the network that will match the structure of each category of support to facilitate the effective transmission of that support. It is important to note that, although previous application of the expanded organizational contingency theory and the task-specific model have not investigated the problematics of requests for support, the network support-specific model treats requests as distinct tasks.[30] Accordingly, support hypotheses in this analysis are distinguished according to requests and provisions of support. All the hypotheses are informed by the descriptions of the model's five dimensions, the structure of the network, and the characteristics of the three categories of support. The methods used to measure and operationalize each dimension are described, and analyses are conducted matching network and support structures according to each dimension. Finally, these findings are reviewed in light of each hypothesis, and optimal matching is discussed.

HYPOTHESES

A summary table (Table 6.1) of all hypotheses is initially presented to provide clarity. Symbols are used in the table in the following manner: A plus indicates that higher levels of a dimension are predicted to be associated with more support; a minus shows that lower levels are predicted to be associated with more support; and a zero cell signifies a dimension and a support are unrelated. For level of dedication, higher levels indicate actors with high levels of dedication and lower levels actors with low levels of dedication. With degree of intimacy, higher levels indicate dyads with strong degrees of intimacy and lower levels dyads with weak degrees of intimacy. For reciprocity, higher levels indicate dyads that are symmetric and lower levels dyads that are asymmetric. With size, higher levels indicate messages sent to large size groups and lower

Table 6.1. Hypothesized Relationships Matching Structural Dimensions of Electronic Social Network Characteristics With Online Social Support Characteristics

Social support category	Level of dedication	Degree of intimacy	Reciprocity	Size[a]	Commonality of major cancer role
Emotional support					
Requested	0	+	+	–	–
Provided	+	+	+		–
Informational support					
Requested	–	0	0	+	0
Provided	+	–	–		0
Companionship					
Requested	+	+	+	–	+
Provided	+	+	+		+

[a]There are no hypothesized relationships for the dimension of size and the provision of support because of the limitations of these data described in detail in the section titled Size in the following.

levels indicate messages sent to small size groups. Finally, for commonality of major cancer role, higher levels indicate dyads that share similar cancer roles and lower levels dyads that share dissimilar cancer roles. The statement of each hypothesis and its rationale follow the table.

Emotional Support

The supracategory of emotional support is made up of five subcategories: understanding/empathy, encouragement, affirming/validation, sympathy, and caring/concern. Requesting any kind of emotional support can make actors feel vulnerable and is more likely to occur in relationships where actors have established a trusting relationships in which they feel safe opening up to one another. Furthermore, because actors would not want to expose themselves and open up to those who might ignore their cry for help, they are apt to request emotional support from actors they know are invested and committed to the relationship evident in their reliable rate of response. These kinds of needs are also more likely to be expressed to a small number of actors who the sender feels secure confiding in and receiving a response from rather than broadcast to the entire Forum. Messages requesting certain kinds of emotional support convey the need for reassurance and positive feedback. This kind of uncertainty often arises for members in dealing with those in their face-to-face networks who occupy a dissimilar cancer role and have an experience different from their own. Caregivers will rely on the judgment of online patients who experience the disease from the same perspective as the cancer sufferer at home to validate actions they feel unsure about, and vice versa.

> **Hypothesis E 1:** Messages containing requests for emotional support are more frequently sent to small size groups, between dyads that share strong degrees of intimacy, symmetric ties, and dissimilar cancer roles, than to large size groups, between those who share weak degrees of intimacy, asymmetric ties, and similar cancer roles.

The provision of all kinds of emotional support requires attention and dedication and is more likely to come from actors who are invested and committed to a relationship. This can be seen in the volume and reliability of their responses. Regular monitoring of most posts also demonstrates the kind of attention and dedication required to know when another member is in need of emotional support. Additionally, it is likely that the kind of devotion inherent in a caregiver's face-to-face role with a patient will carry over to online interactions.

> **Hypothesis E 2:** Messages providing emotional support are sent more frequently by actors with high levels

> of dedication, and within dyads that share high degrees of intimacy, symmetric ties, and dissimilar cancer roles, than by actors who have low levels of dedication, and within dyads that share low degrees of intimacy, asymmetric ties, and similar cancer roles.

Informational Support

Informational support is composed of advice, referrals, and teaching. Messages requesting any kind of informational support are likely to come from actors who do not frequently monitor or interact on the Forum. Some of these actors are new to the experience and do not have much firsthand knowledge of how to manage cancer, whereas others have not benefited from the knowledge regularly posted to the Forum because they do not read posts regularly. Furthermore, requests for very specific information benefits from being sent to a large number of people, increasing the likelihood that someone who has had the experience will read the message and be able to supply the necessary information. These requests are not very sensitive in nature and as such are suitable for broadcast e-mails.

> **Hypothesis I 1:** Messages requesting informational support are sent more frequently to large size groups, by actors with low levels of dedication, than to small size groups, by actors with high levels of dedication.

Actors who continually monitor the Forum are most likely to provide informational support because they read most messages. Such actors are prone to providing a response to messages that are broadcast to the entire list out of dedication to this service the Forum provides. Moreover, informational support does not take a large investment of attention or time to provide and is easily provided in a one-off message to someone with whom an actor has not previously become emotionally involved or even communicated with.

> **Hypothesis I 2:** Messages providing informational support are sent more frequently by actors with high levels of dedication, and within dyads that share weak degrees of intimacy and asymmetric ties, than by actors with low levels of dedication, and within dyads that share strong degrees of intimacy and symmetric ties.

Companionship

Companionship is made up of chatting, humor/teasing, and groupness. Posts that request companionship contain questions regarding topics not related to cancer. This kind of support moves beyond the expressed purpose of the Forum; thus actors who send such posts must have an established, intimate rapport. In addition, because these questions are usually part of an ongoing conversation, they necessitate regular frequent contact and a continuous give-and-take. These requests also tend to be directed to specific actors for these reasons. Finally, actors often form deep bonds with their peers who share a similar cancer experience and naturally move their relationships on the Forum into areas beyond the discussion of cancer.

> **Hypothesis C 1:** Messages requesting companionship are sent more frequently to small size groups, by actors with high levels of dedication, and within dyads sharing strong degrees of intimacy, symmetric ties, and common cancer roles, than to large size groups, by actors with low levels of dedication, and within dyads sharing weak degrees of intimacy, asymmetric ties, and dissimilar cancer roles.

Companionship is provided in messages that progress beyond the Forum's principal topic of cancer and, therefore, requires a great degree of familiarity and an established rapport. It is more likely that actors who have frequent contact will develop a familiarity that allows them to divulge more about themselves than just the aspects affected by cancer. The give-and-take that is necessary to carry on an online dialog made up of the mutual exchange of messages comes from an established rapport. Lastly, actors experiencing cancer in the same way relate to each in a manner that allows their relationship to expand into other areas of their lives.

> **Hypothesis C 2:** Messages providing companionship are sent more frequently by actors with high levels of dedication, and within dyads that share strong degrees of intimacy, symmetric ties, and similar cancer roles, than by actors with low levels of dedication, and within dyads sharing weak degrees of intimacy, asymmetric ties, and dissimilar cancer roles.

Model Dimensions—Operationalization and Analysis

UCINET 6 and SPSS nonparametric tests are used to conduct the following analyses because of two fundamental characteristics of network data. First, network data are made up of all the ties within a population, rather than a random sample of ties from the population. Second, network data are relational, and, therefore, all things are dependent upon one another. Hence, the basic assumptions of most standard statistical procedures are violated and cannot correctly be applied to these data. The statistical procedures in UCINET are created in light of these characteristics, and although many of them reflect procedures commonly used in the social sciences, they are modified to accurately analyze network data. Nonparametric tests similarly do not require these basic assumptions be met. The one exception is the analysis of variance (ANOVA) test, which, although not strictly a nonparametric test, has been shown to be "fairly 'robust' against [i.e., insensitive to] violations of the assumptions of normal distribution" (Abelson, 1995, p. 60, see also Sawilowsky & Blair, 1992).

Operationalization of Dimensions

Isolates and Missing Values

Two procedures are carried out on the data before any of the dimensions are operationalized. Initially four isolates, actors who did not have a connection to the larger network,[31] are removed from the matrices, leaving a population of 80 members. Next, missing values are recoded as such. Values considered missing are those cells where there was no message sent between actors in the message matrix. The data in these cells are not missing in the traditional sense of the word, that is the data are not lacking or unknown, it is known that these actors chose not to connect with one another. Nonetheless these are treated as missing values because the lack of a message between two actors dictates that there can be no support exchanged.

Level of Dedication

This dimension is a property of the individual actor and is measured by tabulating the total number of days a member posted over the 14-day period and then classifying him as a frequent or sporadic poster. A high level of dedication is indicated by frequent activity that is characterized by posting on 7 or more days out of the sample 14-day period, whereas a low level of dedication is sporadic participation identified by posting on 6 days or fewer. Seven days of posting is used as the cutoff point for frequent activity because it represents half the total number of days in the sample. Seventeen members have a high level of dedication and 63 a low level.

Degree of Intimacy

Degree of intimacy is a property of the dyad that is a dimension shared by two members. It is measured by the strength of ties between two actors based on the number of e-mails exchanged.

The number of messages dyads exchanged ranged from 0 to 44. To designate a cutoff point to distinguish between strong and weak ties, the median and mean of the sample are calculated. Because the sample is highly skewed toward weak relationships, the mean of 3.93 is considered a better measure of central tendency than the median of 2. Thus an exchange of 4 messages is used as the upper threshold for weak ties, and dyads that exchanged 5 or more messages are classified as having strong ties. All in all, 54 dyads are categorized as having strong ties representing a high degree of intimacy, and 177 as having weak ties indicating a low degree of intimacy.

Reciprocity

Reciprocity is measured by the balance of messages sent between two actors. It is a property of the dyad that is calculated by reviewing the number of messages passed between actors to determine whether their exchange is symmetric or asymmetric. Naturally, when actors provide one another with exactly the same number of messages, the relationship is considered symmetric. If the exchange is not perfectly even, the actor who sends fewer messages must send at least half the number of the first for the relationship to be considered symmetric. Dyads in which one actor transmits less than half the number of messages the other sent or does not respond at all are designated asymmetric. There are 12 dyads in which the first actor sends two messages and the second actor sends only one. In this case, although the exchange may appear asymmetric, the dyads are classified as sharing a symmetric relationship. This is because of the nature of conversational flow. In each of these dyads, the messages exchanged between the actors consist of an initial message, followed by a response, and then a final post completing the discussion. The completion of an episode of conversation with the exchange of three messages is very common in e-mail communication. It is substantively distinct from an unbalanced dialog and is not accurately represented as an asymmetric tie. In total there are 103 symmetric or reciprocal dyads[32] and 128 that are asymmetric.

Size

The dimension of size in the network support-specific model is unique in two ways: It is a property of each message, and it is only measured on requests for support. Size assesses whether the active members of each support network predominantly contact small groups of actors or large groups of actors when requesting that specific support. To do so, it is necessary to measure whether more messages requesting a particular support were sent to small or large numbers of actors. Because size is a property of each support message, it is not a feature that can be attributed to an actor or dyad consistently throughout the analyses. For example, any actor, regardless of whether he or she possess a high or low degree of dedication, can direct one message to a small size group of actors and broadcast another to the entire Forum. Thus size is not a characteristic of an actor but of a particular message. The second unique aspect of size is that it is only measured on requests for support because, although support is found to be requested of both small and large groups, it is nearly always provided in messages that are directed to only one individual or a small group of individuals. There are some exceptions were teaching and jokes are sent out in broadcast messages. However, the great majority of provisions are sent in messages directed to one or a few individuals creating little variation in the data in regard to provisions of support and the dimension of size. Thus, even though theoretically size might play a role in the provision of support, the proposition cannot be empirically explored with these data.[33]

To measure the dimension of size, the number of messages requesting support that are directed to particular individuals and the number sent out in broadcast messages to the whole Forum are tallied for each support network. Those messages sent to particular individuals are classified as being requested of small size groups and broadcast messages as being requested of large size groups. No directed requests are addressed to more than five people, and only two reach that amount.[34] Across all categories of support, 316 messages are directed to small size groups of actors, and 108 messages are broadcast to large size groups.

Commonality of Major Cancer Role

Commonality of major cancer role is a dimension that is initially measured on the individual but is truly a property of the dyad, that is, an actor's major cancer role must first be determined, but the dimension itself then focuses on whether the role is shared by two actors and if the transmission of support is patterned by similar or dissimilar roles. To do so, members' postings are reviewed to identify each actor's relationship to cancer. Four categories are found on the Forum: cancer patient, caregiver,[35] adult child of patient, and relative or friend of patient. Relatives and friends of cancer patients are relegated to the same category after a review of their messages reveals a great similarity in sentiment and content. This may stem from the fact that there is a similar combination of emotional and physical distance from the cancer patient for a relative and a friend, as opposed to a parent or a caregiver. Each member is placed in one of the five categories, giving 22 patients, 10 caregivers, 14 adult children of patients, and 11 friends or relatives of patients. A final category not listed in the foregoing contains the remaining 23 actors who posted to the Forum with messages regarding cancer but did not specify their relationships to it. These were coded as missing values and omitted from the analysis.

Analyses of Dimensions

A number of procedures are conducted to assess the influence of these dimensions on requests and provisions of support. First, the magnitude of the effect each dimension has on each category of support is determined using regression techniques. The only exception is the dimension of size, discussed in detail in the following. Next, the significance of each dimension's influence on each category of support is established using two distinct approaches because of the manner in which some of the dimensions are measured. For level of dedication, degree of intimacy, and reciprocity, a series of univariate ANOVA tests are carried out to establish the significance of each dimension's predicted influence on the support categories. These are followed by tables that present the proportion of actors/dyads that have a high or low degree of each dimension and request/provide each support. The relative differences between the effects of each dimension on the three supports are compared, demonstrating whether the predicted direction of the relationship between a dimension and each category of support is found in the data. The ANOVA test is used to establish the significance, and the relative differences in effects are used to evaluate whether the influence of the dimension on the supports follows the predicted direction. These two tests are necessary for these three dimensions because actors with high levels of dedication, and dyads with strong degrees of intimacy and reciprocity send a greater number of messages and will necessarily provide more support of all kinds than those with low levels of dedication, weak degrees of intimacy, and asymmetry. In other words, the way these independent variables are measured is somewhat confounded with the dependent variable (see Appendix C for correlation tables). As such the null hypothesis, which tests for the absence of an effect of dedication, intimacy, and reciprocity, may be misleading as a way of confirming or disconfirming the alternative hypothesis. Using ANOVA and comparing relative differences in effects offers better tests of whether the empirical variation of effects of each dimension across the three kinds of social support matches the theoretical predictions summarized in Table 6.1. The way the final two dimensions of size and commonality of major cancer are measured is completely distinct from the number of messages an actor sends and, therefore, it is possible to test against a null hypothesis of no effect. Thus, for these dimensions *t*-tests are used to establish the significance of their predicted influences on supports.

It is not possible to carry out one multiple regression that incorporates all five dimensions to ascertain the magnitude of the dimensions' effects on supports because of differences in units of analysis. For level of dedication the unit of analysis is the actor, whereas for degree of intimacy, reciprocity, and commonality of major cancer role it is the dyad and with size it is the message. Thus, regressions for level of dedication and each category of support will be performed independently, and QAP regressions for the three dimensions that share the dyad as their unit of analysis will be conducted jointly. Regression analysis cannot be performed for the dimension of size on account of how it is measured, that is, size is a measure of whether a message is sent to a large size group or a small size group. A regression would assess whether instances of requests for a particular support are influenced by a message being sent to a large size group or a small size group. However, given that each instance of support is contained in a message, the two measures are nearly identical. There are a total of 424 request messages and a total of 605 instances of requested support. Of the total number of messages requesting support, only 86 contain[36] more than one instance of support requested and are counted more than once. Thus for the dimension of size, the magnitude of the effect cannot be determined. However, *t*-tests provide ample information to confirm or refute hypotheses predicted by the theory.

To establish the significance of the effects that level of dedication, degree of intimacy, and reciprocity have on supports, ANOVA tests are carried out that test against the appropriate null hypothesis, given the way these dimensions are measured. Rather than a null hypothesis of no effect, ANOVA tests against a null hypothesis that a dimension's influence on all supports is fairly uniform. To that end, ANOVA tests whether a dimension is associated with the amount of support requested or provided and if the size of the effect varies by kind of support. The results demonstrate whether there is a significant difference in a dimension's effect across the three supports. A lack of variation in a dimension's effect on diverse supports demonstrates that the dimension is not specifically required to request or provide any one kind of support as predicted by the model. All in all, six univariate ANOVA tests are conducted using the actors' or dyads' dimension categories and the support content of their messages as the independent variables and the proportion of messages actors or dyads send that contain each support as the dependent variable. A table presenting the average percentage of messages containing each kind of support for both high and low degrees of each dimension is provided to compare the predicted directions of the relationships with the observed directions. Relative differences in a dimension's effect on support that match predicted relationships demonstrate that the patterns of observed relationships are consistent with the predicted patterns of effect sizes.

The *t*-tests used to establish the significance of the effects of commonality of major cancer role and size on supports vary somewhat, given the difference in the unit of analysis for the two dimensions. For commonality of major cancer role, the proportion of dyads that request or provide each category of support and share a major cancer role is compared with the proportion of dyads that share a major cancer role in the entire population. If the proportion of dyads in the sample population (support category) that share a major cancer role significantly varies from the proportion of dyads in the larger population of dyads that share a major cancer role, the dimension commonality of major cancer role is shown to have a salient influence on that support category as predicted. For the dimension of size, the proportion of messages requesting each support category that are sent to large size groups is compared with the proportion of messages in the larger population sent to large size groups. If the proportion of messages in the sample population (support category) that are sent to large size groups significantly varies from the proportion of messages in the larger population of messages that are sent to large size groups, the dimension of size is shown to have a salient influence on that support category as predicted.

Level of Dedication

Initially, a series of regressions are implemented to determine the influence of level of dedication on requests and provisions of supports. To conduct a regression for level of dedication in UCINET, an independent variable vector must be created that identifies each actor as possessing a high or low level of dedication. Each actor is assigned a category for level of dedication, and the vector is created using a dummy variable, with a 1 indicating a high level of dedication and a 0 a low level of dedication. UCINET 6 is used to calculate row sums for each of the six matrices of support categories (requested and provided) to produce a singular vector for each that reflects the number of instances of support posted by each actor. These vectors, made up of the number of instances of support requested or provided by each actor, are used as dependent variables. The "statistics,vector,regression" command of UCINET 6 is used to conduct a regression on the dependent vector of each category of support using the independent vector of level of dedication. This process is repeated six times for each category of support requested and provided. The unit of analysis for this dimension is the individual actor, and there are a total of 80 actors in the sample. The findings for support requests are presented in Table 6.2 and for support provision in Table 6.3. In each of these tables the high level of dedication coefficient demonstrates the mean level increase in requests or provisions of each kind of support for those who have high levels of dedication to the Forum compared with those who have low levels of dedication. So, for example, the mean level of emotional support requested is increased by nearly 8 instances (7.965) for actors who have high levels of dedication compared with those who have low levels of dedication.

Next, it must be assessed whether a high level of dedication is needed to request or provide each support. Two univariate ANOVA tests are used to establish whether level of dedication exerts a statistically significant influence on the categories of support requested and provided. The proportion of messages each actor sends containing each kind of support is determined to carry out

Table 6.2. Regression Equations for Categories of Support Requested and Level of Dedication—Measured on the Individual

Social support category requested	Number of active actors[a]	Model fit R^2	High level of dedication[b]
Emotional support	22	.315*	7.965
Informational support	62	.226*	1.835
Companionship	25	.176*	13.362

Note. $N = 80$ actors.
[a]Active actors are those actors who send at least one instance providing a specified kind of support. Inactive actors are those actors who do not send even one instance providing a specified kind of support and are not represented in the table.
[b]A high level of dedication indicates actors who have posted to the Forum on seven or more days out of the 14-day period.
$*p < .000$

Table 6.3. Regression Equations for Categories of Support Provided and Level of Dedication—Measured on the Individual

Social support category provided	Number of active actors[a]	Model fit R^2	High level of dedication[b]
Emotional support	31	.412*	43.469
Informational support	24	.250*	17.490
Companionship	33	.303*	46.739

Note. $N = 80$ actors.
[a]Active actors are those actors who send at least one instance providing a specified kind of support. Inactive actors are those actors who do not send even one instance providing a specified kind of support and are not represented in the table.
[b]A high level of dedication indicates actors who have posted to the Forum on seven or more days out of the 14-day period.
$*p < .000$

the ANOVA. A univariate ANOVA is then performed using the proportion of messages actors send containing each support as the dependent variable, and actors level of dedication and each kind of support as the independent variables. A significant F-statistic for the interaction term for level of dedication and kind of support demonstrates that the null hypothesis of no difference in level of dedication's effect on type of support is discredited. The F-statistics for the interaction term for requests and provisions of supports and level of dedication are 27.150 ($p < .000$) and 2.318 ($p < .10$), respectively.

Finally, the relative differences in the effects level of dedication has on each support are compared in light of the predicted effects to determine whether the predicted direction of the relationship between a dimension and each category is found in the data (Tables 6.4 and 6.5). Theoretical predictions are confirmed when the pattern of relative difference in the observed effect sizes is consistent with the predicted pattern. However, the predictions made for level of dedication and provisions of support do not vary, so the power of this measure is attenuated. Therefore, it is not possible to empirically assess with a great degree of certainty whether the direction of the observed influence level of dedication exerts on the provision of support is consistent with the predicted direction. Nonetheless, this is not the case for level of dedication and requests for support, nor the remaining two dimensions that use this method for assessment. Table 6.4 shows that for level of dedication and support requested the predicted relationships can be characterized as the dimension having no effect on emotional support compared with informational support, where having a high level of dedication has a negative effect, and companionship, where having a high level of dedication has a positive effect. The relative differences in percent displayed in Table 6.4 demonstrate that having a high level of dedication has on average a very small influence on requests for emotional support, with a difference in percent of just 7, a large negative impact on informational support, and a relatively large positive influence on companionship compared with emotional support. These relative differences support the theoretically predicted relationships between level of dedication and requests for supports because the difference in percent between having a high level of dedication and low level of dedication for those requesting emotional support (7) is relatively small compared with companionship (10). Comparing the effects of a high level of dedication on requests for these two supports shows that the impact the dimension makes on emotional support is negligible compared with the positive impact it makes on companionship. The large negative impact that a high level of dedication makes on requests for informational support demonstrates that relative to other supports having a low level of dedication greatly influences requests for this support.

Table 6.4. Percentage of Messages Requesting Support by Actors' Levels of Dedication Including Results for ANOVA Significance Test—Measured on the Actor

Social support category requested	High level of dedication	Low level of dedication	Difference in percent	Theoretical prediction
Emotional support	11	4	7	0
Informational support	6	66	–60	–
Companionship	17	7	10	+

Notes. The *F*-statistic for the ANOVA is 27.150, $p < .000$. $N = 80$ actors.

Table 6.5. Percentage of Messages Providing Support by Actors' Levels of Dedication Including Results for ANOVA Significance Test—Measured on the Actor

Social support category provided	High level of dedication	Low level of dedication	Difference in percent	Theoretical prediction
Emotional support	53	12	41	+
Informational support	26	8	18	+
Companionship	51	18	33	+

Notes. The *F*-statistic for the ANOVA is 2.318, $p < .100$. $N = 80$ actors.

Degree of Intimacy, Reciprocity, and Commonality of Major Cancer Role

One multiple regression including all three of these dimensions can be conducted to determine the influences of the dimensions on requests and provisions of supports because degree of intimacy, reciprocity, and commonality of major cancer role are all properties of the dyad. A matrix is created for each dimension using dummy variables to differentiate the two categories of each dimension to conduct the regressions. For degree of intimacy, a 1 is placed in each cell, representing a dyad that shares a strong degree of intimacy, and a 0 is placed in each cell, representing a dyad that shares a weak degree of intimacy. Similarly, for reciprocity a 1 indicates a symmetric dyad and a 0 an asymmetric dyad. For commonality of major cancer role a 1 indicates a dyad sharing a similar cancer role and a 0 a dyad sharing a dissimilar cancer role. All three of these matrices are then included in a UCINET QAP regression as independent variables, with the matrix of one support category as the dependent variable. This process is repeated a total of six times, once for each of the three support category matrices requested and provided. The dimensions included in these regressions must be kept in a form where the dimension is shared by both members because they are all properties of the dyad and cannot be attributed to any one member. The QAP regression function in UCINET "regress[es] a dependent matrix on one or more independent matrices" (Borgatti et al., 2002), performing a regression while also maintaining the dyadic nature of the dimensions. The unit of analysis for these procedures is the dyad. The sample contains 462 directed dyads, which is the total number of dyads in the sample, where at least one message is sent from one actor to the other. The findings are presented in Table 6.6 (support requested) and Table 6.7 (support provided). In these tables a dimension's coefficient indicates the mean level increase for each kind of support requested or provided for dyads that share that dimension. For instance, dyads that share strong degrees of intimacy demonstrate a mean level increase of requests for emotional support of nearly 1 (.901) versus those dyads that share weak degrees of intimacy. In Tables 6.6 and 6.7 the significance levels for the model fit are produced by the regression procedure.

In addition to calculating the degrees to which the dimensions affect the categories of support, it is also necessary to establish whether each dimension's impact on each category of support is by chance. In other words, which, if any, of these three dimensions are needed to request or provide each support? For degree

Table 6.6. QAP Regression Equations for Categories of Support Requested and Degree of Intimacy, Reciprocity, and Commonality of Major Cancer Role—Measured on the Dyad

Social support category requested	Number of active directed dyads	Model fit R^2	Degree of intimacy	Reciprocity	Common major cancer role
Emotional support	64	.161*	.901	.354	-.180
Informational support	33	.094*	.244	.093	-.048
Companionship	110	.267*	1.486	.271	.203

Note. $N = 462$ directed dyads.
$^*p < .000$

Table 6.7. QAP Regression Equations for Categories of Support Provided and Degree of Intimacy, Reciprocity, and Commonality of Major Cancer Role—Measured on the Dyad

Social support category provided	Number of active directed dyads	Model fit R^2	Degree of intimacy	Reciprocity	Common major cancer role
Emotional support	246	.390*	3.738	1.050	–.721
Informational support	148	.075*	.929	–.057	–.140
Companionship	234	.365*	4.650	.855	.506

Note. $N = 462$ directed dyads.
$^*p < .000.$

of intimacy and reciprocity, ANOVA tests are used to established significance, whereas *t*-tests are used for commonality of major cancer role. The proportion of messages each actor sends containing each kind of support is determined to carry out the ANOVA tests. A univariate ANOVA is performed using the proportion of messages dyads send containing each support as the dependent variable, and dyads' degree of intimacy/reciprocity and each kind of support as the independent variables. A significant *F*-statistic for the interaction term for degree of intimacy/reciprocity and kind of support demonstrates that the null hypothesis of no difference in the dimension's effect on type of support is discredited. The *F*-statistics for the interaction term for requests and provisions of supports and degree of intimacy are 3.070 ($p < .05$) and 9.694 ($p < .000$), respectively. The *F*-statistics for the interaction term for requests and provisions of supports and reciprocity are 4.123 ($p < .05$) and 32.772 ($p < .000$), correspondingly.

Finally, the relative differences in the effects degree of intimacy/reciprocity has on each support are compared in light of the predicted effects to determine whether the predicted direction of the relationship between a dimension and each category is found in the data (Tables 6.8, 6.9, 6.10, and 6.11). Theoretical predictions are confirmed when the pattern of relative difference in the observed effect sizes is consistent with the predicted pattern. For example, in Table 6.8 the predicted relationships between degree of intimacy and supports requested can be described as the dimension having no impact on requests for informational support, as opposed to a strong degree of intimacy having a positive effect on requests for both emotional support and companionship. Reviewing the relative differences in effects for each category of support shows that degree of intimacy on average exerts nearly no influence on informational support, with a difference in percent of 1, and a strong degree of intimacy has a general positive impact on both emotional support and companionship, with a difference in percent of 7 and 11, respectively. These relative differences support the theoretically predicted relationships between degree of intimacy and requests for supports.

The *t*-tests carried out to establish the significance for commonality of major cancer role compare the proportion of dyads that request or provide a category of support and share a major cancer role with the proportion of dyads in the entire population of dyads that share a major cancer role. The null hypothesis is confirmed

Table 6.8. Percentage of Messages Requesting Support by Dyads' Degree of Intimacy Including Results for ANOVA Significance Test—Measured on the Dyad

Social support category requested	Strong degree of intimacy	Weak degree of intimacy	Difference in percent	Theoretical prediction
Emotional support	15	8	7	+
Informational support	5	4	1	0
Companionship	25	14	11	+

Notes. The *F*-statistic for the ANOVA is 3.070 $p < .05$. $N = 462$ directed dyads.

Table 6.9. Percentage of Messages Providing Support by Dyads' Degree of Intimacy Including Results for ANOVA Significance Test—Measured on the Dyad

Social support category provided	Strong degree of intimacy	Weak degree of intimacy	Difference in percent	Theoretical prediction
Emotional support	61	60	1	+
Informational support	17	40	–23	–
Companionship	61	55	6	+

Notes. The *F*-statistic for the ANOVA is 9.694, $p < .000$. $N = 462$ directed dyads.

Table 6.10. Percentage of Messages Requesting Support by Dyads' Reciprocity Including Results for ANOVA Significance Test—Measured on the Dyad

Social support category requested	Symmetric ties	Asymmetric ties	Difference in percent	Theoretical prediction
Emotional support	16	2	14	+
Informational support	6	3	3	0
Companionship	22	9	13	+

Notes. The *F*-statistic for the ANOVA is 4.123, $p < .05$. $N = 462$ directed dyads.

Table 6.11. Percentage of Messages Providing Support by Dyads' Reciprocity Including Results for ANOVA Significance Test—Measured on the Dyad

Social support category provided	Symmetric ties	Asymmetric ties	Difference in percent	Theoretical prediction
Emotional support	64	53	11	+
Informational support	20	57	–37	–
Companionship	60	51	9	+

Notes. The *F*-statistic for the ANOVA is 32.772, $p < .000$. $N = 462$ directed dyads.

if the proportion of dyads that request or provide a category of support and share a major cancer role does not significantly deviate from the proportion of dyads in the larger population that share a major cancer role. Two vectors are created in UCINET 6 to carry out each *t*-test. The first vector contains 462 rows representing all dyads in the entire population and a number of rows representing the number of dyads that provide or request each category of support and share a major cancer role. The two categories of dyad are coded as dummy variables, with a 1 placed in each of the first 462 rows, representing the entire population of dyads, and a 0 placed in the remaining rows, representing each category's population of dyads that share a major cancer role. The second vector contains the same number of rows as the first, but the cells are filled differently. The dyads in the first 462 rows representing the entire population are classified as sharing a major cancer role or not using a dummy variable such that a 1 indicates the former and a 0 the latter. The dyads in the remaining rows representing each category of support are also classified as sharing a major cancer role or not using a dummy variable in the same manner. UCINET 6 uses these vectors to conduct *t*-tests that compute the proportion of dyads that share a similar cancer role for each category of support and the proportion of dyads that share a similar cancer role for the entire population of dyads. A one-tailed *t*-test is then employed to determine whether there is a statistically significant difference between the two proportions. The proportions and the significance levels are presented in Table 6.12 for requests and Table 6.13 for provisions. The omitted category in each table is that of dyads that share a dissimilar cancer role and request or provide support.

Size

Size is the only dimension that is a property of the message and will therefore vary with each message. The aim of the analysis is to determine whether the proportion of messages sent to large size groups for each category of support significantly differs from the proportion of messages sent to large size groups in the entire population. To that end, first the proportion of messages sent to large size groups for each category of support is established. Next the proportion of messages sent to large size groups for the entire sample population is calculated. Then, three one-tailed t-tests are conducted to compare the proportion of messages sent to large size groups for each category of support with the proportion of messages sent to large size groups for the larger population of

Table 6.12. Percentage of Dyads That Share a Common Major Cancer Role and Request Support Including *t*-Tests for Significance—Measured on the Dyad

Social support category requested	Common major cancer role
Emotional support	41
Informational support	30
Companionship	46***

Note. $N = 462$ directed dyads.
*$p < .05$
**$p < .01$
***$p < .005$

Table 6.13. Percentage of Dyads That Share a Common Major Cancer Role and Provide Support Including *t*-Tests for Significance—Measured on the Dyad

Social support category provided	Common major cancer role
Emotional support	34
Informational support	24
Companionship	41***

Note. $N = 462$ directed dyads.
*$p < .05$
**$p < .01$
***$p < .005$

all messages. Each *t*-test demonstrates whether the proportion of messages sent to large size groups for the support category deviates significantly from the proportion of messages sent to large size groups for the larger population. The null hypothesis of no effect for the specified type of support cannot be rejected if the proportion of messages sent to large size groups for each category of support does not significantly deviate from the proportion of messages sent to large size groups for the larger population. The UCINET command "statistics, vector, *t*-test" is used to carry out the *t*-tests. For each *t*-test one vector is created containing 424 rows representing messages requesting support for the entire sample and a number of rows representing the number of messages requesting support for each category of support. The second vector contains the same number of rows as the first, but the cells are filled differently. The messages in the first 424 rows representing the entire population are classified as being sent to a large or small size group using a dummy variable such that a 1 indicates a large size group and a 0 a small size group. Messages in the remaining rows representing each category of support are also classified as being sent to a large or small size group using a dummy variable in the same manner. A one-tailed *t*-test is then used to determine whether there is a statistically significant difference between the proportion of messages sent to large size groups for each category of support and the proportion of messages sent to large size groups for the larger population of all messages. The proportions and significance levels are presented in Table 6.14. The omitted category in each table is that of messages that are sent to small size groups and request support.

FINDINGS

For the purpose of clarity, Table 6.15 presents the hypothesized and observed relationships matching network characteristics with categories of support based on the results of the foregoing analyses. The first symbol in each cell represents the hypothesized relationship, and the second symbol that follows the slash mark represents the observed relationship. As with Table 6.1, symbols are used in the table in the following manner: A plus indicates that higher levels of a dimension are predicted to be associated with more support; a minus shows that

Table 6.14. Percentage of Messages That Are Sent to Large Size Groups and Request Support Including *t*-Test Results for Significance—Measured on the Message

Social support category requested	Large size groups
Emotional support	14**
Informational support	58***
Companionship	18*

Note. $N = 424$ messages.
*$p < .05$
**$p < .01$
***$p < .000$

Table 6.15. Hypothesized and Observed Relationships Matching Structural Dimensions of Electronic Social Network Characteristics With Online Support Characteristics

Social support category	Level of dedication	Degree of intimacy	Reciprocity	Size[a]	Commonality of major cancer role
Emotional support					
Requested	0/0	+/0	+/+	–/–	–/0
Provided	+/+	+/0	+/+		–/0
Informational support					
Requested	–/–	0/0	0/0	+/+	0/0
Provided	+/+	–/–	–/–		0/0
Companionship					
Requested	+/+	+/+	+/+	–/–	+/+
Provided	+/+	+/+	+/+		+/+

[a]There are no hypothesized or observed relationships for the dimension of size and the provision of support because of the limitations of these data described in detail in the section titled Size.

lower levels are predicted to be associated with more support; and a zero cell signifies a dimension and a support are unrelated. The original hypothesized relationship is supported when the predicted association between a dimension and support matches the observed relationship.

Emotional Support

> **Hypothesis E 1:** Messages containing requests for emotional support are more frequently sent to small size groups, between dyads that share strong degrees of intimacy, symmetric ties, and dissimilar cancer roles than to large size groups, between those who share weak degrees of intimacy, asymmetric ties, and similar cancer roles.

The findings support the predictions made in Hypothesis E 1 regarding requests for emotional support and the dimensions of reciprocity and size but not degree of intimacy and commonality of major cancer role. Reciprocity is shown to have a statistically significant effect on dyads' likelihood of exchanging requests for emotional support as predicted. Dyads sharing symmetric ties request an average of .354 more instances of emotional support than those sharing asymmetric ties. Size exerts a salient influence on the transmission of this support such that a significantly larger proportion (86%) of messages are sent to small size groups containing requests for emotional support than the proportion (75%) of messages that are sent to small size groups in the larger population of request for support ($p < .01$). Conversely, the dimensions of degree of intimacy and commonality of major cancer role are not found to have a statistically significant impact on requests for emotional support as predicted.

> **Hypothesis E 2:** Messages providing emotional support are sent more frequently by actors with high levels of dedication and within dyads that share high degrees of

> intimacy, symmetric ties, and dissimilar cancer roles than by actors who have low levels of dedication and within dyads that share low degrees of intimacy, asymmetric ties, and similar cancer roles.

The results support the prediction made in Hypothesis E 2 regarding the provision of emotional support and the dimensions of level of dedication and reciprocity but not for degree of intimacy and commonality of major cancer role. Level of dedication is found to exert a significant influence on the provision of emotional support such that having a high level of dedication increases the average number of instances of this support provided by nearly 44 compared with having a low level. Reciprocal relationships also have a significant influence on the provision of emotional support such that symmetric dyads exchange on average one instance more than do asymmetric dyads. The dimensions of degree of intimacy and commonality of major cancer role are not found to have a statistically significant impact on requests for emotional support as predicted.

Informational Support

> **Hypothesis I 1:** Messages requesting informational support are sent more frequently to large size groups, by actors with low levels of dedication, than to small size groups, by actors with high levels of dedication.

The results fully support Hypothesis I 1 regarding the predicted relationships between requests for informational support and the dimensions of level of dedication and size. Level of dedication is found to exert a significant influence on requests for informational support such that having a low level of dedication increases the mean amount of informational support requested by nearly two instances versus a high level. With the dimension of size, the proportion (58%) of messages sent to large size groups containing requests for informational support is significantly larger than the proportion (25%) of messages that are sent to large size groups in the larger population of requests for support ($p < .000$).

> **Hypothesis I 2:** Messages providing informational support are sent more frequently by actors with high levels of dedication, and within dyads that share weak degrees of intimacy and asymmetric ties, than by actors with low levels of dedication, and within dyads that share strong degrees of intimacy and symmetric ties.

The relationships between the provision of informational support and the dimensions of level of dedication, degree of intimacy, and reciprocity are confirmed as predicted in Hypothesis I 2. Possessing a high level of dedication has a significant influence on this support, with such actors providing on average about 18 more instances of informational support than those with low levels of dedication. Dyads that share weak degrees of intimacy result in a significant mean increase of .929 instances of informational support provided compared with pairs that have strong degrees of intimacy. Reciprocity exhibits a statistically significant influence on the provision of this support as predicted, although the impact of sharing an asymmetric tie only increases the mean level of informational support provided by .057.

Companionship

> **Hypothesis C 1:** Messages requesting companionship are sent more frequently to small size groups, by actors with high levels of dedication, and within dyads sharing strong degrees of intimacy, symmetric ties, and common cancer roles, than to large size groups, by actors with low levels of dedication, and within dyads sharing weak degrees of intimacy, asymmetric ties, and dissimilar cancer roles.

The findings support the predicted relationships in Hypothesis C 1 regarding requests for companionship and the dimensions of level of dedication, degree of intimacy, reciprocity, size, and commonality of major cancer role. Level of dedication is found to have a statistically significant influence on request for companionship as predicted, with actors who have a high level of dedication requesting on average roughly 14 more instances of this support than those with a low level. Degree of intimacy demonstrates a statistically significant impact on this support as predicted such that dyads sharing strong degrees of intimacy show a nearly 1.5 times increase in the mean instances of companionship requested compared with pairs that have weak degrees of intimacy. Reciprocity has a statistically significant influence, leading to an increase in the average instances of companionship requested of .271 for dyads sharing symmetric ties versus asymmetric ties. The effect of sharing a similar major cancer role boosts the mean amount of companionship requested by .203, which is found to be significant. Finally, size has a statistically significant impact on requests for companionship as predicted. The proportion (82%) of messages sent to small size groups containing requests for companionship is significantly larger than the proportion (75%) of messages that are sent to small size groups in the larger population of requests for support ($p < .05$). The relationship presented in Table 6.14 for requests for companionship and the dimension of size represents the proportion of messages sent to large size groups that request this support (18%), which is the converse of the relationship regarding messages sent to small size groups and requests for companionship.

> **Hypothesis C 2:** Messages providing companionship are sent more frequently by actors with high levels of dedication and within dyads that share strong degrees of intimacy, symmetric ties, and similar cancer roles, than by actors with low levels of dedication and within dyads

sharing weak degrees of intimacy, asymmetric ties, and dissimilar cancer roles.

The findings are in agreement with the predicted relationship in Hypothesis C 2 regarding the provision of companionship and the dimensions of level of dedication, degree of intimacy, reciprocity, and commonality of major cancer role. Actors who have high levels of dedication provide a statistically significant average of nearly 47 more instances of companionship than do those with low levels. The relationship between the provision of companionship and degree of intimacy is statistically significant, demonstrating that dyads sharing strong degrees of intimacy provide a mean increase of almost 5 instances of this support in contrast to those sharing weak degrees. Reciprocal relationships are found to have a statistically significant influence on the provision of companionship, with symmetric dyads providing an average of .855 more instances of support compared with asymmetric ones. The effect of sharing a similar major cancer role significantly increases the mean amount of companionship provided by .5.

Discussion

A number of overarching phenomena emerge from the data in matching the structural characteristics of the electronic social network with those of the supportive tasks along the five dimensions of the network support-specific model. The dimension of level of dedication makes a strong impact on most kinds of support, with the exception of requests for emotional support. High levels of dedication characterized by frequent contact with the Forum tend to be most influential, apart from for requests for informational support, where low levels of dedication are more salient. Requests for informational support are more common among actors possessing a low level of dedication, characterized by infrequent contact with the Forum. Actors do not invest much time in the Forum when their purpose for accessing the group is simply to request informational support. Requests for emotional support are not greatly influenced by actors' levels of dedication, whereas requests for companionship tend to come from those with high levels of dedication. On the other hand, having high levels of dedication is shown to increase the kinds and amounts of support a member is likely to provide across the board. Actors who make frequent contact with the Forum clearly do the job of supporting those who need it, whatever kind of support they may require. Companionship is the only kind of support where high levels of dedication impact both requests and provisions of support. Actors need to spend more time interacting with other members to exchange this most personalized of all three supports.

The dimension of degree of intimacy does not exert as significant an effect as level of dedication, but it does influence the provision of informational support and companionship in general. Informational support is provided more often between dyads that share weak degrees of intimacy. This is consistent with the finding regarding level of dedication that those actors who interact less often on the Forum are more likely to request informational support whereas those who interact most often are more likely to provide informational support. Dyads made up of one actor who makes little contact with the Forum and another actor who makes a lot of contact are not likely to have a great deal of interaction with one another and will not develop a strong degree of intimacy. In addition, requesting informational support does not require a great deal of personal investment or cost and, as such, is suited to a relationship that is not very intimate. The dimensions' strongest association is with companionship, where possessing strong degrees of intimacy, as opposed to weak ones, impacts both requests and provisions of support. Sharing strong degrees of intimacy is most important when it comes to moving relationships beyond discussing cancer to the chatting, humor, and teasing that characterizes companionship. To do so requires the kind of confidence and rapport that comes from strong ties built on recurrent interaction. Conversely, informational support is exchanged more often between dyads sharing weak ties and does not require a strong intimate relationship at all. Emotional support falls somewhere between the two and is not influenced by whether dyads share strong or weak ties. It seems that emotional support can be both requested and provided within dyads regardless of whether they share intimate ties or not. This may not be surprising on a forum that is meant to provide support for those experiencing cancer. In this context, emotional support is probably considered common currency rather than a sensitive sentiment that can only be shared after an intimate relationship has been developed.

The dimension of reciprocity exerts an influence on all supports except for requests for informational support. Informational support is, however, most often provided within dyads that share asymmetric ties, further demonstrating that this support does not require an established relationship of any kind. On the other hand, sharing symmetrical ties plays an important role in requesting and providing both emotional support and companionship. Intimate relationships may not play a significant role in whether or not actors exchange emotional support on the Forum, but they are more likely to request and provide it within reliable balanced relationships. Companionship is also requested and provided most often within dyads sharing symmetric ties. The give-and-take nature of the subcategories of chatting and humor makes this kind of support best suited to balanced relationships.

The dimension of size is unique in being a property of each support network rather than an actor or a dyad, as well as in only being measured on requests for support. Size exerts a significant influence on requests for all supports. Informational support stands out for a fourth time as demonstrating the opposite effect of the other two supports, that is, messages requesting informational support are more likely to be sent to large size groups, whereas requests for emotional support and companionship are sent most often to small size groups. Requests for this impersonal factual-based support need not be personally directed to a specific person or small group of people and benefits from being sent to a large group. The best strategy for searching for problem-solving and educational information is increasing the likelihood of an accurate and effective response by asking as many people as possible. Unlike face-to-face networks, the technology of an online forum makes it just as easy to ask one member as it is to ask them all. Conversely, actors tend to keep their requests for emotional support and companionship limited to a smaller group of actors. Actors may not need a great deal of established intimacy to request emotional support, but they do direct their messages to specific actors rather than broadcasting them to the entire group. The nature of this support falls between the factual quality of informational support and the familiar character of companionship. Requests for companionship are also directed to a few select actors because progressing to topics beyond cancer requires that actors have an established confidence that is not usually shared by a large number of actors.

Commonality of major cancer role is the dimension that has the smallest impact on the transmission of support. The only support it has an effect on is companionship. Sharing a similar or dissimilar major cancer role does not influence who actors request emotional and informational supports from or who they provide it to. Thus those who share both similar and dissimilar roles are able to exchange these two forms of support freely. Companionship tends to be requested and provided more often within dyads that share similar cancer roles than those sharing dissimilar roles.

Actors who experience the disease in the same way develop more of a peer identity and camaraderie compared with those who cannot know firsthand how it feels to be in the same position. This allows their relationships to develop into friendships that extend beyond the cancer experience.

Conclusion

Overall, the network support-specific model correctly predicted a match between the structure of this electronic social network and the online support transmitted within it, with 23 out of 27 potential matches. The model accurately predicted the kind of online support that was either requested or provided, given certain electronic social network features 85% of the time. The previous chapters document the kinds of online support found on the Forum and demonstrate the general patterns of support exchanged. The application of the network support-specific model now clarifies precisely how and why online support is exchanged within the SOL-Cancer Forum. Thus, the analysis presented in these two final chapters provides a detailed understanding of the transmission of social support on the online Forum by describing the kinds of participants who request and provide different supports and explaining why this is the case.

CHAPTER 7

CONCLUSION

The broad purpose of this research was to extend the study of social support into the realm of an online environment. The specific aims were to uncover the social support found in the SOL-Cancer Forum and the social structure that developed in its electronic social network to clarify how and why social support was transmitted within it. To that end, discussions of the SOL-Cancer Forum were analyzed using several diverse methods. The results of these analyses provide deep insight into the kinds of support exchanged on the Forum, members' interactions in the electronic network, and the relationship between them. The implications of the study inform a number of disciplines in contributing a detailed investigation of online social support, CMC and electronic social networks, and, ultimately, how they all come together in an Internet forum.

After an introduction to the research in Chapter 1, the second chapter focused on the incidence of online social support to demonstrate that members of the Forum exchange social support in an online environment through CMC. A wide range of support in large quantities was documented. Emotional support was found is five distinct forms, whereas informational support and companionship were each observed in three forms. In view of the 11 subcategories of support found in messages exchanged on the Forum and the volume of support they amount to, there can be no question as to whether the CMC contained on the SOL-Cancer Forum is capable of transmitting social support, both of the factual kind and, in greater quantities, the personal kind. The members of SOL-Cancer Forum have all met through the Forum, and nearly all their interactions are conducted online, yet their supportive activities are clearly not inhibited by the lack of physical proximity or face-to-face contact. Thus, the very precise forms in which emotional support and companionship are documented and the great quantity of each recorded in a brief two-week period firmly challenge the notions put forth by the social presence model and the reduced social cues models that a lack of intimacy (in CMC) and a tendency toward negative interactions create an environment ill-suited for social interaction or the sharing of emotions (Baron, 1984; Short et al., 1976; Stoll, 1995).

The third and fourth chapters examined the Forum's social structure and its effect on the transmission of social support using social network analysis. The analyses consisted of identifying actors' positions in the electronic social network, the roles they play in relation to one another, and how that creates the Forum's social structure, which in turn influences how support is exchanged. The initial findings presented in the first network chapter characterize actors as divided into two general positions, the givers and the takers, whose respective roles are as members who contribute posts to the Forum and those who simply receive messages without reciprocating. All kinds of social support in varying amounts are exchanged within this social structure between the givers. On the other hand, the takers only receive informational support in limited quantities.

The second network chapter delves deeper into the network's social structure to further differentiate the activity of the givers beyond the simple classification of actors who contribute to the Forum. The givers all consider each other SOLers, but their levels of participation in the Forum differ greatly. Four actor categories emerge from the SOLers to capture the different positions they occupy and roles they play in the network. The star actor is the most active in the network and occupies the leadership role of supporting the greatest number of actors. She is also the focal actor in receiving support. The next category is made up of the prime givers, who are the second most active members. They are positioned behind the leader, and, although they provide the other SOLers with a large amount of support, their primary role is supporting the star actor. The serious members also have a high level of participation, albeit lower than the star and prime givers. They constitute the main bulk of SOLers who contribute messages regularly and provide as much support as they receive. Finally, the moderate users post to the group with the lowest frequency of all the SOLers and have a small but steady presence. They are on the fringes of the SOLers, and even though they have relationships with the others, they are not as highly integrated into the group. In addition to the SOLers, the Forum also contains another category of actor labeled the takers because they do not contribute any support to the Forum and simply receive it.

Once all the actors were categorized according to their positions in the network and the network's social structure was established this chapter moved on to analyzing the transmission of support within the network structure. The findings show that the depth and breadth of relationships that develop within and between positions impact the kinds and amounts of support the actors who occupy them share with one another. The star, prime givers, and serious members regularly interact a great deal, develop intimate relationships, and exchange all kinds of support in the largest amounts. The moderate users participate less often, form some relationships, and receive smaller amounts of emotional support and informational support but no companionship. Finally, the takers post no directed messages, are not at all integrated into the network, and only receive informational support. These findings demonstrate that participating in the Forum more often facilitates the development of more profound relationships, which results in the transmission of greater quantities and kinds of support. The number of SOLers that exhibit this pattern calls into question Cummings, Butler, and Kraut's (2002) finding that there was no significant association between frequency of contact and psychological closeness with an Internet partner.

The final two chapters employed the expanded organizational contingency theory to move the analysis another step further and explain why social support was exchanged in this manner. To that end, the task-specific model that provides a concrete method with which to apply expanded organizational contingency theory to the data was modified to suit an electronic social network and online social support, resulting in the network support-specific model. This model was then used to generate six hypotheses, that predicted the network characteristics that would match different support characteristics to facilitate the transmission of support. Hypothesis testing demonstrated that the model correctly specified 23 out of 27 matches. Thus the model presented a detailed explanation of how and why online support is transmitted in an electronic social network by clarifying the network features associated with requests and provisions of support. In doing so, the network support-specific model provides a tool with which to assess the support potential of other online groups. This can impart more insight as to the benefits and limitations of various kinds of online groups than Cummings, Sproull, and Kiesler's (2002) broad statement that "[l]istservs are not as good as small [face-to-face] groups for … gaining social support"(p. 107).

Overall, this research provides a comprehensive understanding of online social support on an Internet forum and elaborates a number of methods that may be applied to this pursuit in other online groups. The second chapter constructed a coding scheme for online social support that documents the presence of social support on the SOL-Cancer Forum, the forms it takes, and the volume with which it occurs. The next two chapters demonstrated the use of social network techniques to describe the social structure that developed in the Forum's electronic social network and illustrated how support moved throughout it. The final two chapters developed a network support-specific model that clarifies why social support is transmitted in this manner and provides a framework that can be applied to other electronic social networks to identify how and when support will be requested and provided. All told, this research greatly satisfies the call for "current research … to develop new measures of computer-mediated support and … how social support is enacted in online groups" (p. 329) that Cotton (2001) put forth in her article reviewing the implications of Internet technology for the field of medical sociology.

Limitations of the Study and Future Directions

The first limitation to the scope of this study is the social support received by lurkers. As cited by Nonnecke and Preece (2003a, p. 129), "more than 55% of the (discussion list) members lurked with no posts" and as stated by Barry Wellman (Nonnecke & Preece, 2003b, p. 125), "lurking is normal, it is the people who post who are abnormal." Thus, without the ability to gather and analyze data on the nonpublic participants of the SOL-Cancer Forum it is not possible to determine what support, if any, was transmitted to them. Nor can it be established whether these analyses conducted on support exchanged among active posters accurately reflects the distribution of social support to SOL members on the whole or merely the nature of provision among the "abnormal" few who actual post. Future research into the support received by nonpublic members of online support groups could reveal the true extent of the quantity of social support provided by these groups and supply a novel realm of data to which the network support-specific model could be applied.

Another finding from Nonnecke and Preece's (2003c) study of lurkers is that some lurkers reported making contact with individuals from the group through side-posts. This finding highlights a second limitation to the research. Not only lurkers but all SOL members have the capability to contact each other through side-posts regarding discussions that begin on the Forum. Each message posted to the Forum contains the private e-mail address the actor used to become part of the group. Hence, there is the potential for support to have been exchanged between SOL members during the sample period that is not contained in these data. As a fellow researcher pointed out, "how do you know the one-time posters don't send Elle a private thank you?" (Benjamin Forman, personal communication, May 2004). Unfortunately, this proposition cannot be empirically explored with these data. Conducting a similar analysis of the discussions of an online forum coupled with a questionnaire including queries regarding side-posts and the support they provide could supply the data necessary to satisfy such queries.

Distributing a questionnaire would also provide an avenue with which to measure the efficacy of the support received on the Forum that was not within the scope of these data. Actors who participate in the group could be asked to express their perception of the usefulness of the support received and their satisfaction with receiving support from the group. Questions could also be included from established scales that assess individuals' levels of loneliness and depression. This kind of measure would be most effective if an initial questionnaire could be distributed to actors when they first participate and a second survey administered after they were members for a certain period of time.

A fourth area in which it would be beneficial to extend this work is in conducting a dynamic analysis. The complete collection of raw data from which the two-week sample was selected contains all messages posted to SOL-Cancer Forum from 1995 to 2000. A variety of longitudinal analyses using this time period in different ways could be performed. Conducting analyses similar to those included in this work on samples selected from different periods over time could reveal if the findings from this research persist. Analyses could also be performed to evaluate any changes that may have occurred in the manner in which actors participated and exchanged support as the Internet grew in use over the five-year period.

One final, and possibly most salient, limitation of this research is the inability to analyze the relationship between actors' online activities and offline relationships. Using time-diary data on Internet use and face-to-face interactions, Nie and Hillygus (2002) have found evidence supporting "displacement" theory that time spent online takes time away from interacting face-to-face with family and friends. "For every hour spent on the Internet at home, the model suggests, individuals are spending an average of almost 30 fewer minutes with their families. … The relationship is identical, though substantively weaker, for time spent with friends and for time spent on social activities" (p. 9). Kraut et al. (1998) argue that this could be detrimental to individuals' social well-being if actors are swapping strong ties (face-to-face) for weak ties (online) and call for an assessment of the quality of online ties versus offline ties. In contrast, Kestnbaum, Robinson, Neustadtl, and Alvarez (2002) compared the time diaries of Internet users versus nonusers and found no statistical difference between the two populations in regard to time spent on specific social activities and a slightly higher amount of time spent on in-home and away socializing for Internet users. The author assert that "Internet use seems more a 'time enhancer,' one in which people do not seem forced to give up other activities to accommodate it. Indeed, it may function like home appliances and the telephone, allowing one to be more productive in use of time … ." (p. 37). Wellman and Hampton (1999) argue that although some researchers assume time spent on the Internet is taking time away from meaningful face-to-face relationships, "…it is more likely pulling people away from sitting by themselves in front of the television watching Seinfeld reruns" (p. 651). It is not possible to evaluate if the time members are dedicating to the SOL-Cancer Forum is having an effect on their face-to-face interactions without possessing data regarding participants' offline relationships.

An additional concern raised by not having access to data regarding actors' offline networks is the inability to assess whether the support these actors receive online is augmenting face-to-face support, taking away from face-to-face support, or filling a need for support lacking in face-to-face networks. Kraut et al. (1998) propose two contrasting models, a "rich get richer" model pronouncing that those who already possess satisfying offline support networks get more benefit from online support and a "social compensation" model where those lacking in offline support garner the support they need online. A third possibility is that those with effective face-to-face support networks may begin to rely more heavily on support received from the online group and turn away from family and friends supplying support offline. For example, Mickelson (1997) compared two populations of parents of children with special needs, those who used traditional face-to-face networks for support and those who used electronic support groups. She found those parents who used electronic support groups evaluated their family and friends as less supportive regarding their child's disability than those who relied on traditional networks. This begs the question, Did these parents withdraw or reach out? Many scholars have shown how access to online support liberates individuals from the limitations of physical place, time, appearance, and stigma, allowing them ongoing access to peer support and marking the end of social isolation during difficult periods (Boberg et al., 1995; Davison et al., 2000; Gustafson et al., 1993; Korenman & Wyatt, 1996; Rodgers & Chen, 2005; Winzelberg, 1997). However, what is the cost? Helgeson, Cohen, Schulz, and Yasko (2000) report that women with breast cancer who had a high level of emotional support from their partner previous to participation in a peer discussion group experienced an adverse affect on physical functioning from partaking in the group, although theirs is not a study conducted on an online support. These questions must be resolved before online support venues can be used for their true potential benefits.

Implications of the Study

The ever-growing presence and adoption of the Internet has fueled the creation of increasing numbers of online support groups that cater to a wide variety of health-related needs. These groups have the potential to provide the benefits of social support conveyed in traditional face-to-face groups without traditional limitations of material resources, proximity, and temporality. The ease of access afforded by an online support group facilitates the possibility for physically debilitated and geographically dispersed patients to participate at their convenience. The limited material and organizational resources they require make online social support groups practical for hospitals or patients to create and maintain. This work offers a detailed understanding of how and why an online support group functions in providing social support, allowing this beneficial resource, which is both easily accessible and time and cost efficient, to be optimally used by those in need.

Online support groups can offer benefits to patients whose limited physical resources create obstacles to attending face-to-face groups at a time when any factor that positively affects health and well-being is crucial. Peer support groups provide cancer patients with a safe outlet for expressing feelings of anger, grief, and hopelessness with others who have been there, rather than placing an addition emotional burden on family members and friends. These groups also give patients an opportunity to feel empowered by helping someone else in providing empathy, encouragement, advice, and useful information. However, a great obstacle to cancer patients' using peer support groups is the tremendous fatigue and consequent dependence on friends and family that results from chemotherapy treatments. Membership in online support groups can be maintained with a few keystrokes performed from the sick bed, furnishing cancer patients with the opportunity to obtain and provide peer support whenever it is needed and convenient for them. They can be freed from the constraints of only being able to participate in a support group on a specific day and time when they may be too ill or weak to partake. Moreover, participation does not require assistance from already burdened friends or family with such things as grooming or transportation, providing patients with a sense of empowerment by enabling them to carry out a task autonomously. In short, online cancer support groups may provide a means for sick individuals to obtain the benefits of a kind of social support they cannot get from friends and family without requiring the same expenditure of resources that face-to-face groups do.

This research has examined the discussions of cancer patients, their caregivers, and family and friends in an online support forum and has clarified the nature of support that is requested and provided in a group that lacks face-to-face interaction and physicality. This online Forum has been shown to supply its participants with a great variety and amount of support. Moreover, it has demonstrated the kind of participation that elicits different forms of support. Public policy that aims to foster health and well-being in such populations can benefit from the clarity provided by this work on how online social support functions. Policy makers can decide if and when to encourage patients and doctors to explore online support as an additional form of treatment. Practical outcomes could include a list of online cancer support groups published by various medical organizations and routinely distributed by doctors to encourage patients to explore this option for social support. Patients who receive chemotherapy treatments on an outpatient basis, as is becoming increasingly common, could receive support at home through an online support group run by the hospital and monitored by a nurse. Face-to-face groups that meet on oncology floors could add online counterparts to provide continuous support for patients who are in and out of the hospital with rounds of chemotherapy. A webcam could transmit face-to-face meetings to those at home in real time or in a video clip that can be accessed on the Web site when patients are up to it. The cost of such technology is continually decreasing and is not prohibitively costly for hospitals to obtain. Including a discussion board on the Web page would offer those at home the ability to contribute during the meeting or add to the discussion at another time. Alternatively, patients who feel uncomfortable with face-to-face interactions could have the opportunity to gain the benefits of peer support by contributing to a group that offers anonymity or by simply lurking. Overall, the varied implications of this research, which delves into issues of online social support, electronic social networks, online communities, and CMC, are relevant to a number of disciplines that study these subjects, such as, communication studies, epidemiology, psychology, social work, and sociology.

Appendix A

Operational Measures of the SOL Coding Scheme—Final Version

- **Emotional support**
  - **Understanding/Empathy**
    - **Requested**—Searching for someone who has an appreciation for or can identify with one's experience or feelings often, but not necessarily because of having had a similar experience. Examples include the following:
      - ✓ I wonder if others who have had the same surgery as I have are experiencing pain? Please let me know.
      - ✓ Is anyone else having problems regaining their energy. By May it will be a year since I finished treatments and I still feel tired a lot of the time.
      - ✓ And then of course, the Dr never calls with results—we always have to wait till his next appt.
    - **Provided**—Appreciating and/or identifying with what someone is expressing often, not necessarily, based on having shared a similar experience. Examples include the following:
      - ✓ I know how you feel.
      - ✓ Yes, it is so very hard to watch a loved one in such pain.
      - ✓ I also had a temporary colostomy and was reconnected a year ago.

- **Encouragement**
  - **Requested**—Expressing despair and/or the need to feel hopeful or courageous. Examples include the following:
    - ✓ They say hopefully it will buy us a year but there is no hope of a cure.
    - ✓ It makes me very sad to think that Mom will not be here to see my son grow up. I try & not think too much about it but she's not eating and her eyes are so sad. They do light up with my son though and I just need to keep concentrating on the positive.
    - ✓ I wish to God I could find something at last that causes this rare thing and finally knock it out. I know she is tired of being treated and stuck with needles often. She just needs to heal and rest and that is so difficult when this thing keeps raging.
  - **Provided**—Attempts to inspire hope and courage, to hearten. All prayers. Examples include the following:
    - ✓ I've seen people beat this before.
    - ✓ I'll keep you in my prayers.
    - ✓ Good luck with your test.
    - ✓ Messages with inspirational stories.
- **Affirming/Validating**
  - **Requested**—Expressing uncertainty and/or a need for positive feedback for a difficult course of action, attitude, or decision. Examples include the following:
    - ✓ Last night we had a long discussion on what she considers "quality" of life. My thoughts were as long as we are able to communicate with each other, then that

should be fine!!! Of course, I am not the one who is having to do all this chemo and pills and throwing up and so on. It could be so much worse for her. We did agree on the premise of as long as she is not in a lot of pain and in her right mind, she would continue with this chemo.

✓ I just told him like it is, no holding back on him. Explained that he can continue to keep his head in the sand and depend on others to do their job, or take control of his own life and by the way didn't he need to do his will? I was not a softy with him, no coddling.

- **Provided**—Acknowledgement and/or positive reinforcement of someone, their ideas, attitude, or actions. Complimenting. Examples include the following:

✓ Well said.

✓ You're a winner.

✓ I believe that you are 100% on the right course

- **Sympathy**

- **Requested**—Expressing sorrow or regret for one's own situation. Examples include the following:

✓ No kidding about how you can go from the top of the ride to nearly crashing.

✓ My concern is that we have tried and experienced so much for Mary that she is getting tired of being poked and attending these clinics.

✓ I'd love to see (the pity pot) as I seem to need it a lot.

- **Provided**—Expressing sorrow for or feeling troubled by another's situation. Examples include the following:

✓ I'm sorry the surgery was so tough.

✓ My heart goes out to you for what you're enduring.
✓ It's terrible that your mom was treated that way.

- **Caring/Concern**
  - **Requested**—Expressing a need for a great amount of attention and general support either directly or indirectly by sharing bad news.
    ✓ I'm real scared and this has helped. … I need help.
    ✓ It has been confirmed that my husband has bone mets. .. I am in a fog.
    ✓ I got a call late last night that they are now thinking it is more than an infection and that Tommy may have relapsed.
  - **Provided**—Demonstrating regard for someone's well-being by being very attentive and interested. Examples include the following:
    ✓ I'll be thinking of you.
    ✓ I've always looked for your posts and love hearing what you are up to.
    ✓ I'm happy to hear that your life has returned to normal.

➢ **Informational support**

- **Advice**
  - **Requested**—Asking for guidance or advice. Examples include the following:
    ✓ She will appreciate any advice.
    ✓ Any/all suggestions welcome.
    ✓ I was wondering if there is any other way to prevent this?
  - **Provided**—Giving guidance and/or making suggestions. Examples include the following:

- ✓ Try to suggest she conserve energy as much as possible to build up strength. Let everyone take care of her.
- ✓ I can't stress enough to go with your instincts about things.
- ✓ You have to go in as a warrior and FIGHT!

- **Referrals**
  - **Requested**—Inquiring about a source for information or assistance. Examples include the following:
    - ✓ Do you know of a site I might find some answers to my particular case.
    - ✓ Do any of you know an endocronologist or onco that knows or understands MTC (medullary thryroid cancer)?
    - ✓ Where do you buy digestive enzymes and what are they called?
  - **Provided**—Offering a source for information or assistance. Examples include the following:
    - ✓ Another site is Memorial Sloan Kettering Cancer Center. Their site is http://www.mskcc.org.
    - ✓ I buy from Donna Splain at tahitian noni juice.com.
    - ✓ Dr. Susan Love has a good book about it and probably a website.

- **Teaching**
  - **Requested**—asking for instructional and/or education information. Examples include the following:
    - ✓ I could use the colon-cancer nutrition info too—can't find the original msg.
    - ✓ I am wondering why the doctors are letting so much time go by…

- ✓ If chemo goes throughout the entire body, why is radiation necessary on top of it?

- **Provided**—passing on instructional and/or educational information. Examples include the following:
  - ✓ I took Xanax and Ativan for the anxiety, morphine for the pain, Ambien to sleep at night.
  - ✓ Myelofibrosis—its cause is unknown. A chronic but progressive disease characterized by fibrosis (thickening and scaring) of the bone marrow, which leads to anemia and the presence of immature red and white blood cells in the circulation.
  - ✓ Thalidomide is marketed under the name Thalomid by Celgene Co.

➢ **Companionship**

- **Chatting**
  - **Requested**—asking questions regarding a topic that is NOT about cancer. Examples include the following:
    - ✓ What part of Canada are you from?
    - ✓ Could you do an old lady a favor and tell me what Vicci's son's name is?
    - ✓ Isn't it awful when you've run out excuses to do housework?
  - **Provided**—a thread of conversation that is NOT about cancer. Examples include the following:
    - ✓ You know John, I watched an old movie to get into the spirit of the snowfall last night.
    - ✓ I find candles very peaceful and was going thru a ton of them, so I started making my own... I LOVED IT!

✓ Just a quick note, I have finally made it to America, having a lovely time in Sherman Oaks, CA.

- **Humor/teasing**
  - **Requested**—sending a joke, personally kidding. Examples include the following:
    - ✓ George W. Bush, in an airport lobby, noticed a man in a long flowing white robe with a long flowing white beard and flowing white hair…
    - ✓ Now Auntie, do I have to tell everyone about the time that you sat on it so long that you got a ring mark! I saw it with my own two eyes when she mooned me… we called it moon over Manhattan ;+) Gotch ya!
    - ✓ John, you little brat.
  - **Provided**—laughing, sending a joke, personally kidding. Examples include the following:
    - ✓ LOLOLOLOLOLOL!!!!!
    - ✓ Every year, the fairy of Joy visits the earth and who ever she touches with her wand receives HAPPINESS! May she beat the shit out of you!
    - ✓ Happy Birthday Marty and if you go streakin don't forget to iron your Birthday Suite!!!
- **Groupness**
  - **Requested**—asking permission to participation in the group, asking someone to join or respond to the group and/or the group's Web site. Examples include the following:
    - ✓ Let us know how it goes.
    - ✓ When can you tell us of your treatment and about the trial?

- ✓ I hope you stay in touch with this forum for I believe there are many who could benefit from your involvement.

- **Provided**—Addressing the group, referring to benefits or actions of the group and/or the group's Web site. Examples include the following:
  - ✓ Dear Friend(s),
  - ✓ Hi, Everyone:
  - ✓ The mol prayers have been so comforting to me.
  - ✓ We are all pulling for you.

Appendix B

Table B.1
Emotional Support Collapsed Matrix—Five Categories

	Star	Prime givers	Serious members	Moderate users	Takers
Star	0	63	77	36	22
Prime givers	101	114	119	69	12
Serious members	77	87	89	21	11
Moderate users	18	34	18	8	9
Takers	0	0	0	0	0

Table B.2
Informational Support Collapsed Matrix—Five Categories

	Star	Prime givers	Serious members	Moderate users	Takers
Star	0	17	30	10	59
Prime givers	23	30	47	12	21
Serious members	13	31	32	10	14
Moderate users	3	10	1	1	8
Takers	0	0	0	0	0

Table B.3
Companionship Collapsed Matrix—Five Categories

	Star	Prime givers	Serious members	Moderate users	Takers
Star	0	114	114	40	13
Prime givers	155	172	103	41	6
Serious members	92	81	64	13	2
Moderate users	8	23	13	7	2
Takers	0	0	0	0	0

Table B.4
Emotional Support Density Matrix—Five Categories

	Star	Prime givers	Serious members	Moderate users	Takers
Star		10.500	7.700	2.400	0.458
Prime givers	16.833	3.800	1.983	0.767	0.042
Serious members	7.700	1.450	0.989	0.140	0.023
Moderate users	1.200	0.378	0.120	0.038	0.013
Takers	0.000	0.000	0.000	0.000	0.000

Table B.5
Informational Support Density Matrix—Five Categories

	Star	Prime givers	Serious members	Moderate users	Takers
Star	2.833	3.000	0.667	1.229	
Prime givers	3.833	1.000	0.783	0.133	0.073
Serious members	1.300	0.517	0.356	0.067	0.029
Moderate users	0.200	0.111	0.007	0.005	0.011
Takers	0.000	0.000	0.000	0.000	0.000

Table B.6
Companionship Density Matrix—Five Categories

	Star	Prime givers	Serious members	Moderate users	Takers
Star		19.000	11.400	2.667	0.271
Prime givers	25.833	5.733	1.717	0.456	0.021
Serious members	9.200	1.350	0.711	0.087	0.004
Moderate users	0.533	0.256	0.087	0.033	0.003
Takers	0.000	0.000	0.000	0.000	0.000

Appendix C

Table C.1
Correlation Coefficients for Categories of Support Requested and Level of Dedication—Measured on the Individual*

Social support category requested	Level of dedication
Emotional support	.561
Informational support	.475
Companionship	.419

*Significance levels are not generated by UCINET 6 for this measure.

Table C.2
Correlation Coefficients for Categories of Support Provided and Level of Dedication—Measured on the Individual*

Social support category provided	Level of dedication
Emotional support	.642
Informational support	.500
Companionship	.550

*Significance levels are not generated by UCINET 6 for this measure.

Table C.3
Correlation Coefficients for Categories of Support Requested and Degree of Intimacy—Measured on the Dyad

Social support category requested	Degree of intimacy
Emotional support	.378*
Informational support	.290*
Companionship	.505**

*$p < .10$
**$p < .05$
***$p < .000$

Table C.4
Correlation Coefficients for Categories of Support Provided and Degree of Intimacy—Measured on the Dyad

Social support category provided	Degree of intimacy
Emotional support	.600**
Informational support	.268*
Companionship	.591**

*$p < .10$
**$p < .05$
***$p < .000$

Table C.5
Correlation Coefficients for Categories of Support Requested and Reciprocity—Measured on the Dyad

Social support category requested	Reciprocity
Emotional support	.291
Informational support	.221
Companionship	.334

*$p < .10$
**$p < .05$
***$p < .000$

Table C.6
Correlation Coefficients for Categories of Support Provided and Reciprocity—Measured on the Dyad

Social support category provided	Reciprocity
Emotional support	.418*
Informational support	.112
Companionship	.390*

*$p < .10$
**$p < .05$
***$p < .000$

Table C.7
Correlation Coefficients for Categories of Support Requested and Commonality of Major Cancer Role—Measured on the Dyad

Social support category requested	Commonality of major cancer role
Emotional support	.039
Informational support	.030
Companionship	.187

*$p < .10$
**$p < .05$
***$p < .000$

Table C.8
Correlation Coefficients for Categories of Support Provided and Commonality of Major Cancer Role—Measured on the Dyad

Social support category provided	Commonality of major cancer role
Emotional support	.052
Informational support	.011
Companionship	.205

*$p < .10$
**$p < .05$
***$p < .000$

Notes

1. The Forum's name and the names of its members have been changed to protect anonymity.
2. A third aspect of social support that was discussed and researched at this time was the underlying process by which social support affects health. Findings showed that social support operated through an enacted process and a perceived one. Because these data contain only enacted support, this will not be discussed here. For further discussion see Gottlieb (1985) and Dunkel-Schetter and Bennet (1985).
3. There is a body of social support literature that does not consider companionship a form of support distinct from emotional support. However, while observing this online forum, it has become clear that companionship is not only distinct from emotional support but is a significantly large component of social support on the Forum. Thus, for my purposes it will not be subsumed under another type of support.
4. The first four dimensions of the model are fashioned to capture the salient structural features of groups and tasks. The final three dimensions are included specifically to differentiate between tasks best suited to a primary group versus a formal organization.
5. For an empirical test of the organizational contingency theory see Chapter 5 or Litwak et al. 1989.
6. This is not the case for some research done on online support groups set up for the purpose of research that contain less than 10 members. See Weinberg's research.
7. This is most often the case in forums that fall int o the category of Computer-Supported Social Networks but not necessarily in Computer-Assisted Social Networks (see Note 8 for definition of Computer-Assisted Social Networks).
8. The types of electronic social network that an actor can access can be divided into two overarching categories: Computer-Supported Social Networks (CSSNs) and Computer-Assisted Social Networks (CASNs) (Wellman, et al. 1996). CSSNs are characterized by a set of actors whose ties are created and maintained through electronic connections. These ties many be extended to include phone conversations or face-to-face interactions, but they are established through electronic connections and primarily, if not solely, maintained through electronic interactions. SOL-Cancer Forum is a CSSN. CASNs, on the other hand, are traditional social networks based on face-to-face interactions

that are extended to include electronic communication like e-mail, organization listservs, and chat lines for extended classroom discussion (Wellman, et. al. 1996). Some forms of electronic communication readily lend themselves to both, for example, e-mail and e-groups.

9. Based on the content of messages, there are a very small number of instances when members of the Forum have meet face-to-face. This actual physical contact accounts for a tiny fraction of all social interactions.
10. The names of the Forum and its members have been changed to protect anonymity.
11. The distinction between categorizing personal experience as emotional support and informational support is described in greater detail in the section titled Designing the SOL Coding Scheme.
12. Activism can be categorized as advice when a particular individual is directed to engage in some form of activism in response to something s/he is personally experiencing. It can be categorized as groupness when all members are asked to engage in activism as a form of group mobilization.
13. Taboo topics may be coded as either chatting or humor/teasing depending on the content of the post.
14. Some researchers would argue that rarely occurring behaviors can be the most interesting subject of study. This was not found in the discussions in the SOL-Cancer Forum during the sample time period. A larger sample period may have produced more interesting findings for this category.
15. Although Braithwaite et al. use the term "network support" rather than "companionship," reviewing the subcategories of this support reveals that it contains dimensions similar to the category of companionship in the SOL scheme.
16. There are a few instances where SOL members write about sending mail or phoning one another.
17. The five subcategories of tangible assistance are not included because the possibility of coding this kind of support was ruled out.
18. All posts are presented exactly as they appear without any corrections made to grammar, spelling, or punctuation.
19. It is expected that requests for support will make up a much smaller percentage of all support on the Forum because support is often provided without being requested because it is inherently the purpose of a support group.
20. ROFLOL stands for Rolling On the Floor Laughing Out Loud. It is used to express great laughter.
21. The mean of this group is 8.87 when calculated without the individual outdegree of Elle, who is an outlier in sending messages to 59 other members, whereas the next nearest member only sends messages to 28 other members. When Elle's binary outdegree is included, the mean of the group is skewed to 10.75.

22. These numbers are based on the givers who are included in the network, therefore excluding the three givers who do not send or receive a message containing companionship.
23. Hierarchical clustering was also used for these purposes but has been omitted from the text because it simply provides additional confirmation to the findings that are already amply demonstrated by the previous two analyses. Information regarding the hierarchical clustering analysis and results are available from the author upon request.
24. Robin is the only actor in this category who receives four more messages than she sends and sends to one member less than she receives from. She is placed within this category nonetheless for two reasons: First, the large volume of messages she sends and receives solidifies her position as one of the primary SOLers; second, she is one of only two members who send a very great number of messages to the group in general, rather than directing them to any one person. Undirected messages, however, are not included in the counts of Freeman Degrees.
25. In addition to the six prime givers, the program also recommends the inclusion of one more actor in the network's core. This actor, Joe, is the first actor in the category of serious members in the network that includes Elle. This is not considered meaningful when discussing the prime givers in the network containing Elle because the significance of Joe's behavior is increased greatly when Elle's acute activity is removed. Thus he is moving into a category he would not occupy in a network containing the star actor.
26. For a discussion of why isolates need to be removed before calculating network centralization see Chapter 3.
27. See Chapter 1 for a detailed discussion regarding the relationship between social support and health, as well as the buffer and direct effects hypotheses.
28. In the event that the two health professional responsible for classifying the causes of death disagree on a ranking, the average ranking is applied.
29. The kind of electronic social network referred to here is a Computer-Supported Social Network (CSSN), defined by Wellman et al.(1996). See Note 8 for discussion.
30. For further explanation see Chapter 5.
31. These four actors are present in the original sample because two of them sent one message to the other two. Neither one of the actors replied, nor did any of the four exchange messages with any other member.
32. A review of the number of dyads that have a weak tie for the dimension of degree of intimacy (177) and the number with a reciprocal tie (103) shows that a tie can be both weak and reciprocal. There are three combinations of the number of messages exchanged that are categorized as both weak and reciprocal: 1:1, 2:2, 2:1 (see text).

33. It is not possible to measure size on provisions of support by counting the number of actors who respond to a request. In doing so, the unit of analysis would change from the message to the actor. Given that requests are measured by the size of the group a message containing a request is sent to, to be consistent and correct, provisions must be measured by the size of the group a message containing a provision is sent to as well.
34. The complete distribution of the number of actors directed messages requesting support are sent to is as follows: 262 sent to one actor, 12 sent to two actors, 5 sent to three actors, and 2 sent to five actors. Thus, directed messages requesting support are coded as being sent to small size groups that range in numbers from one to five actors. Broadcast messages requesting support are sent to all current members, hence a large size group containing roughly 80 actors.
35. Identification as a caregiver supersedes any other familial classification because of the fact that caring for a cancer patient creates a very distinct role in relation to cancer that is more salient than familial relation for these purposes.
36. The breakdown of the 86 request messages that are counted more than once is as follows: 58 messages are counted twice, 23 messages are counted three times, 4 messages are counted four times, and 1 message is counted five times.

REFERENCES

Abelson, R. (1995). *Statistics as principled argument.* Hillsdale, NJ: Lawrence Erlbaum.

Avery, D. (1998). Electronic parenting or, it takes a (listserv) village to raise families with disabilities. *CMC Magazine,* 5.

Barak, A. (2007). Emotional support and suicide prevention through the Internet: A field project report. *Computers in Human Behavior, 23,* 971–984.

Baron, N. (1984). Computer mediated communication as a force in language change. *Visible Language, 18,* 118–141.

Baym, N. K. (1995). The emergence of community in computer-mediated communication. In S. Jones (Ed.), *CyberSociety: Computer-mediated communication and community* (pp. 138–163). Thousand Oaks, CA: Sage.

Baym, N. K. (2000). *Tune in, log on: Soaps, fandom, and online community.* Thousand Oaks, CA: Sage.

Berkman, L. F. (1984). Assessing the physical health effects of social networks and social support. *Annual Review of Public Health, 5,* 413–432.

Berkman, L. F. (1985). The relationship of social networks and social support to morbidity and mortality. In S. Cohen & S. L. Syme (Eds.) *Social support and health* (pp. 241–262). Orlando, FL: Academic Press.

Berkman, L. F. (1986). Social networks, support and health: Taking the next step forward. *American Journal of Epidemiology, 123,* 559–562.

Berkman, L. F., & Breslow, L. (1983). *Health and ways of living : The Alameda County study.* New York: Oxford University Press.

Berkman, L. F., Glass, T., Brissette, I, & Seeman, T. E. (2000). From social integration to health: Durkheim in the new millennium. *Social Science and Medicine, 51,* 843–857.

Berkman, L. F., & Kawachi, I. (Eds.). (2000). *Social epidemiology.* New York: Oxford University Press.

Berkman, L. F., & Syme, S. L. (1979). Social networks, host resistance, and mortality: A nine-year follow-up study of Alameda County residents. *American Journal of Epidemiology, 109,* 186–204.

Boberg, E., Gustafson, D., Hawkins, R., Chien-Lung, C., Bricker, E., Pingree, S., et al. (1995). Development, acceptance, and use patterns of a computer-based education and social support system for people living with AIDS/HIV infection. *Computers in Human Behavior, 11,* 289–311.

Borgatti, S., & Everett, M. (1999). Models of core/periphery structures. *Social Networks, 21,* 375–395.

Borgatti, S., Everett, M., & Freeman, L. (2002). *Ucinet for Windows: Software for social network analysis.* Harvard, MA: Analytic Technologies.

Braithwaite, D., Waldron, V., & Finn, J. (1999). Communication of social support in computer-mediated groups for people with disabilities. *Health Communication, 11,* 123–151.

Brennan, P., Moore, S., & Smyth, K. (1995). The effects of a special computer network on caregivers of persons with Alzheimer's disease. *Nursing Research, 44,* 166–172.

Cassel, J. (1976). The contributions of the social environment to host resistance. *American Journal of Epidemiology, 104,* 107–122.

Chenault, B. (1998). Developing personal and emotional relationships via computer-mediated communication. *CMC Magazine,* 5.

Cobb, S. (1976). Social Support as a Moderator of Life Stress. *Psychosomatic Medicine,* 38, 300–314.

Cobb, S. (1979). Social support and health through the life course. In M. W. Riley (Ed.), *Aging from birth to death: Interdisciplinary perspectives* (pp. 93–106). Boulder, CO: Westview Press.

Cohen, C., Teresi, J., & Holmes, D. (1987). Social networks and mortality in an inner-city elderly population. *International Journal of Aging and Human Development, 24,* 257–296.

Cohen, S., & Wills, T. (1985). Stress, social support and the buffering hypothesis. *Psychological Bulletin, 98,* 310–357.

Costigan, J. (1999). Introduction: Forest, trees, and Internet research. In S. Jones (Ed.), *Doing Internet research : Critical issues and methods for examining the Net* (pp. xvii–xxiv). Thousand Oaks, CA: Sage.

Cotton, S. (2001). Implications of Internet technology for medical sociology in the new millennium. *Sociological Spectrum, 21,* 319–340.

Culnan, M., & Markus, M. L. (1987). Information technologies. In F. M. Jablin, L. Putnam, K. Roberts, & L. Porter (Eds.), *Handbook of organizational communication: An interdisciplinary perspective* (pp. 420–443). Newbury Park, CA: Sage.

Cummings, J., Butler, B., & Kraut, R. (2002). The quality of online social relationships. *Communications of the ACM, 45,* 103–108.

Cummings, J., Sproull, L., & Kiesler, S. B. (2002). Beyond hearing: Where real world and online support meet. *Group Dynamics, 6,* 78–88.

Cutrona, C., & Suhr, J. (1992). Controllability of stressful events and satisfaction with spouse support behaviors. *Communication Research, 19,* 154–174.

Davison, K., Pennebaker, J., & Dickerson, S. (2000). Who talks? The social psychology of illness support groups. *American Psychologist, 55,* 205–217.

Degenne, A., & Forsé, M. (1999). *Introducing social networks.* London: Sage.

Dohrenwend, B., Dohrenwend, B., Dodson, M., & Shrout, P. (1984). Symptoms, hassels, social support, and life events: Problems of confounded measures. *Journal of Abnormal Psychology, 93,* 222–230.

Dunham, P., Hurshman, A., Litwin, E., Gusella, J., Ellsworth, C., & Dodd, P. (1998). Computer-mediated social support: single young mothers as a model system. *American Journal of Community Psychology, 26,* 281–306.

Dunkel-Schetter, C., & Bennett, T. (1985). Differentiating the Cognitive and Behavioral Aspects of Social Support. In I. Sarason & Sarason, B. (Eds.), *Social support : theory, research, and applications*, (pp. 267–295) Dordrecht ; Boston: M. Nihjoff.

Durkheim, E. (1951). *Suicide, a study in sociology.* Glencoe, IL: Free Press.

Finn, J. (1999). An exploration of helping processes in an online self-help group focusing on issues of disability. *Health and Social Work, 24,* 220–231.

Folkman, S., & Lazarus, R. (1980). An analysis of coping in a middle-aged community sample. *Journal of Health and Social Behavior, 21,* 219–239.

Forman, B. (2004, May). Personal communication.

Freeman, L. (1978). Centrality in social networks conceptual clarification. *Social Networks, 1,* 215–239.

Freeman, L., Roeder, D., & Mulholland, R. (1979). Centrality in social networks: II. Experimental results. *Social Networks, 2,* 119–141.

French, J., Jr., Rogers, W., & Cobb, S. (1974). Adjustment as person-environment fit. In G. Coehlo, D. Hamburg, & J. Adams (Eds.), *Coping and adaptation.* New York: Basic Books.

Friedmann, H. (1988). Form and substance in the analysis of the world economy. In B. Wellman & S. D. Berkowitz (Eds.), *Social structures : A network approach* (pp. 304–326). New York: Cambridge University Press.

Furlong, M. (1989). An electronic community for older adults: The SeniorNet network. *Journal of Communication, 39,* 145–153.

Garton, L., Haythornthwaite, C. A., & Wellman, B. (1999). Studying on-line social networks. In S. Jones (Ed.), *Doing Internet research: Critical issues and methods for examining the Net* (pp. 75–105). Thousand Oaks, CA: Sage.

Gauthier, D., & Chaudoir, N. (2004). Tranny Boyz: Cyber community support in negotiating sex and gender mobility among female to male transsexuals. *Deviant Behavior, 25,* 375–398.

Gore, S. (1978). The effect of social support in moderating the health consequences of unemployment. *Journal of Health and Social Behavior, 19,* 157–165.

Gore, S. (1985). Styles of coping with stress. In S. Cohen & S. L. Syme (Eds.), *Social support and health* (pp. 263–280). Orlando, FL: Academic Press.

Gottlieb, B. H. (1985). Social networks and social support: An overview of research, practice and policy implications. *Health Education Quarterly, 12,* 5–22.

Granovetter, M. (1973). The strength of weak ties. *American Journal of Sociology, 78,* 1360–1380.

Gustafson, D., Hawkins, R., Boberg, E., McTavish, F., Owens, B., Wise, M., et al. (2002). CHESS: 10 years of research and development in consumer health informatics for broad populations, including the underserved. *International Journal of Medical Informatics, 65,* 169–177.

Gustafson, D., Wise, M., McTavish, F., Taylor, J. O., Wolberg, W., Stewart, J., et al. (1993). Development and pilot evaluation of a computer-based support system for women with breast cancer. *Journal of Psychosocial Oncology, 11,* 69–93.

Haines, V., & Hurlbert, J. (1992). Network range and health. *Journal of Health and Social Behavior, 33,* 254–266.

Hall, A., & Wellman, B. (1985). Social networks and social support. In S. Cohen & S. L. Syme (Eds.), *Social support and health* (pp. 23–41). Orlando, FL: Academic Press.

Helgeson, V., Cohen, S., Schulz, R., & Yasko, J. (2000). Group support interventions for women with breast cancer: Who benefits from what? *Health Psychology, 19,* 107–114.

Hinkle, L., Jr. (1974). The effect of exposure to culture change, social change, and changes in interpersonal relationships on health. In B. S. Dohrenwend & B. P. Dohrenwend (Eds.), *Stressful life events: Their nature and effects* (pp. 9–44). New York: Wiley.

Hirsch, B. (1980). Natural support systems and coping with major life changes. *American Journal of Community Psychology, 8,* 159–172.

Hobfoll, S., & Stokes, J. (1988). The process and mechanics of social support. In S. Duck (Ed.), *Handbook of personal relationships* (pp. 497–517). New York: Wiley.

House, J. S. (1981). *Work stress and social support.* Reading, MA: Addison-Wesley.

House, J. S., & Kahn, R. (1985). Measures and concepts of social support. In S. Cohen & S. L. Syme (Eds.), *Social support and health* (pp. 83–108). Orlando, FL: Academic Press.

House, J. S., Robbins, C., & Metzner, H. (1982). The association of social relationships and activities with mortality: Prospective evidence for the Tecumseh Community Health Study. *American Journal of Epidemiology, 116,* 123–140.

House, J. S., Umberson, D., & Landis, K. (1988). Structures and processes of social support. *Annual Review of Sociology, 14,* 293–318.

Jackson, P. (1992). Specifying the buffering hypothesis: Support, strain, and depression. *Social Psychology Quarterly, 55,* 363–378.

Kaplan, B., Cassel, J., & Gore, S. (1977). Social support and health. *Medical Care, 15,* 47–58.

Kestnbaum, M., Robinson, J., Neustadtl, A., & Alvarez, A. (2002). Information technology and social time displacement. *IT & Society, 1,* 21–37.

Kiesler, C. (1985). Policy implications of research on social support and health. In S. Cohen & S. L. Syme (Eds.), *Social support and health* (pp. 347–364). Orlando, FL: Academic Press.

Kim, M.-S., & Bresnahan, M. (1994). A process model of request tactic evaluation. *Discourse Processes, 18,* 344–371.

King, S., & Moreggi, D. (1998). Internet therapy and self-help groups: The pros and cons. In J. Gackenbach (Ed.), *Psychology and the Internet: Intrapersonal, interpersonal, and transpersonal implications* (pp. 77–109). San Diego, CA: Academic Press.

Klemm, P., Hurst, M., Dearholt, S., & Trone, S. (1999). Cyber solace: Gender differences on Internet cancer support groups. *Computers in Nursing 17,* 65–72.

Kling, R. (1996). Social relationships in electronic forums: Hangouts, salons, Workplaces, and communities. In R. Kling (Ed.), *Computerization and controversy: Value conflicts and social choices* (pp. 426–454). San Diego, CA: Academic Press.

Knipscheer, C. P. M., & Antonucci, T. C. (1990). Social network research: Review and perspectives. In C. P. M. Knipscheer & T. C. Antonucci (Eds.), *Social network research: Substantive issues and methodological questions* (pp. 161–173). Amsterdam: Swets & Zeitlinger.

Knoke, D., & Kuklinski, J. (1982). *Network analysis.* Newbury Park, CA: Sage.

Korenman, J., & Wyatt, N. (1996). Group dynamics in an e-mail forum. In S. C. Herring (Ed.), *Computer-mediated communication: Linguistic, social, and cross-cultural perspectives* (pp. 225–242). Amsterdam: J. Benjamins.

Kraut, R., Kiesler, S. B., Boneva, B., Cummings, J., Helgeson, V., & Crawford, A. (2001). Internet paradox revisited. *Journal of Social Issues, 58,* 49–74.

Kraut, R., Lundmark, V., Patterson, M., Kiesler, S. B., Mukopadhyay, T., & Scherlis, W. (1998). Internet paradox: A social technology that reduces social involvement and psychological well-being? *American Psychologist, 53,* 1017–1031.

Landman-Peeters, K., Hartman, C., Van Der Pompe, G., Den Boer, J., Minderaa, R., & Ormel, J. (2005). Gender differences in the relation between social support, problems in parent-offspring communication, and depression and anxiety. *Social Science and Medicine, 60,* 2549–2559.

Lazarus, R. S., & Launier, R. (1978). Stress-related transactions between person and environment. In L. A. Pervin & M. Lewis (Eds.), *Internal and external determinants of behavior.* New York: Plenum Press.

Lea, M., & Spears, R. (1995). Love at first byte? Building personal relationships over computer networks. In J. T. Wood & S. Duck (Eds.), *Under-studied relationships: Off the beaten track* (pp. 197–233). Thousand Oaks, CA: Sage.

Liebler, C., & Sandefur, G. (2002). Gender differences in the exchange of social support with friends, neighbors, and co-workers at midlife. *Social Science Research, 31,* 364–391.

Lin, N., Ensel, W. M., Simeone, R. S., & Kuo, W. (1979). Social support, stressful life events, and illness: A model and an empirical test. *Journal of Health and Social Behavior, 20,* 108–119.

Lin, N., Ye, X., & Ensel, W. M. (1999). Social support and depressed mood: A structural analysis. *Journal of Health and Social Behavior, 40,* 344–359.

Litwak, E. (1985). *Helping the elderly: The complementary roles of informal networks and formal systems*. New York: Guilford Press.

Litwak, E., Messeri, P., Wolfe, S., Gorman, S., Silverstein, M., & Guilarte, M. (1989). Organizational theory, social supports, and mortality rates: A theoretical convergence. *American Sociological Review, 54,* 49–66.

Liu, W. T., & Duff, R. W. (1972). The strength in weak ties. *Public Opinion Quarterly, 36,* 361–366.

Loader, B., Muncer, S., Burrows, R., Pleace, N., & Nettleton, S. (2002). Medicine on the line? Computer-mediated social support and advice for people with diabetes. *International Journal of Social Welfare, 11,* 53–65.

Marsden, P. (1989). Methods for the characterization of role structures in network analysis. In L. Freeman, D. White, & A. Romney (Eds.), *Research methods in social network analysis* (pp. 489–530). Fairfax, VA: George Mason University Press.

Marsden, P., & Campbell, K. E. (1984). Measuring tie strength. *Social Forces, 63,* 482–501.

McCormick, N., & McCormick, J. (1992). Computer friends and foes: Content of undergraduates' electronic mail. *Computers in Health Behavior, 8,* 379–405.

McKenna, K. Y. A., & Bargh, J. A. (1998). Coming out in the age of the Internet: Identity "demarginalization" through virtual group participation. *Journal of Personality and Social Psychology, 75,* 681–694.

Meier, A. (1997). Inventing new models of social support groups: A feasibility study of an online stress management support group for social workers. *Social Work in Groups, 20,* 35–53.

Messeri, P., Silverstein, M., & Litwak, E. (1993). Choosing optimal support groups: A review and reformulation. *Journal of Health and Social Behavior, 34,* 122–137.

Mickelson, K. (1997). Seeking social support: Parents in electronic support groups. In S. B. Kiesler (Ed.), *Culture of the Internet* (pp. 157–178). Mahwah, NJ: Lawrence Erlbaum.

Miyata, K. (2002). Social support for Japanese mothers online and offline. In B. Wellman & C. Haythornthwaite (Eds.), *The Internet in everyday life* (pp. 520–548). Victoria, Australia: Blackwell.

Muncer, S., Burrows, R., Pleace, N., Loader, B., & Nettleton, S. (2000). Births, death, sex and marriage…but very few presents? A case study of social support in cyberspace. *Critical Public Health, 10,* 1–18.

Nie, N., & Hillygus, D. S. (2002). The impact of Internet use on sociability: Time-diary findings. *IT & Society, 1,* 1–20.

Nonnecke, B., & Preece, J. (2003a). Silent participants: Getting to know lurkers better. In C. Lueg & D. Fisher (Eds.), *From Usenet to CoWebs: Interacting with social information spaces* (pp. 110–132). New York: Springer. Quoting B. Mason. Issues in virtual enthnography. In K. Buckner (Ed.), *Ethnographic studies in real and virtual environments.* Edinburgh: Inhabited Information Spaces and Connected Communities.

Nonnecke, B., & Preece, J. (2003b). Silent participants: Getting to know lurkers better. In C. Lueg & D. Fisher (Eds.), *From Usenet to CoWebs: Interacting with social information spaces* (pp. 110–132). New York: Springer. Quoting B. Wellman. (1999). Personal communication, May.

Nonnecke, B., & Preece, J. (2003c). Silent participants: Getting to know lurkers better. In C. Lueg & D. Fisher (Eds.), *From Usenet to CoWebs: Interacting with social information spaces* (pp. 110–132). New York: Springer.

North, C. L. (1998). *Computer-mediated communication and social support among eating disordered individuals: An analysis of the alt.support.eating-disord News Group.* Graduate dissertation, University of Oklahoma.

Orth-Gomer, K. (1994). Individual and environmental resources for health promotion: Interactive effects. *Advances: The Journal of Mind-Body Health, 10,* 29–31.

Parks, M., & Eggert, L. (1991). The role of social context in the dynamics of personal relationships. *Advances in Personal Relationships, 2,* 1–34.

Parks, M., & Floyd, K. (1996). Making friends in cyberspace. *Journal of Computer-Mediated Communication, 1,* article 4.

Pearlin, L. (1985). Social structure and processes of social support. In S. Cohen & S. L. Syme (Eds.), *Social support and health* (pp. 43–60). Orlando, FL: Academic Press.

Pearlin, L., & Aneshensel, C. (1986). Coping and social supports: Their functions and applications. In L. H. Aiken & D. Mechanic (Eds.), *Applications of social science to clinical medicine and health policy* (pp. 417–437). New Brunswick, NJ: Rutgers University Press.

Pew, Internet & American Life Project. (2006). Latest trends: Online activities—Total: Tracking survey (March 2000 to April 2006). http://207.21.232.103/trends/Internet_Activities_1.11.07.htm.

Preece, J., & Maloney-Krichmar, D. (2003). Online communities: Focusing on sociability and usability. In J. Jacko & A. Sears (Eds.), *Handbook of human-computer interaction* (pp. 596–620). Mahwah, NJ: Lawrence Erlbaum.

Preece, J., Nonnecke, B., & Andrews, D. (2004). The top five reasons for lurking: Improving community experiences for everyone. *Computers in Human Behavior, 20,* 201–223.

Radin, P. (2006). To me, it's my life: Medical communication, trust, and activism in cyberspace. *Social Science and Medicine, 62,* 591–601.

Rice, R. (1993). Media appropriateness: Using social presence theory to compare traditional and new organizational media. *Human Communication Research, 19,* 451–484.

Rice, R. (1994). Network analysis and computer-mediated communication systems. In S. Wasserman & J. Galaskiewicz (Eds.), *Advances in social network analysis: Research in the social and behavioral sciences* (pp. 167–203). Thousand Oaks, CA: Sage.

Robinson, J., & Turner, J. (2003). Impersonal, interpersonal and hyperpersonal social support: Cancer and older adults. *Health Communication, 15,* 227–234.

Rodgers, S., and Chen, Q. (2005). Internet community group participation: Psychosocial benefits for women with breast cancer. *Journal of Computer-Mediated Communication, 10,* article 5.

Sagrestano, L., Feldman, P., Rini, C., Woo, G., & Dunkel-Schetter, C. (1999). Ethnicity and social support during pregnancy. *American Journal of Community Psychology, 27,* 869–898.

Sarason, I. G., Sarason, B. R., Shearin, E., & Pierce, G. R. (1987). A brief measure of social support: Practical and theoretical implications. *Journal of Social and Personal Relationships, 4,* 497–510.

Sawilowsky, S., & Blair, R. C. (1992). A more realistic look at the robustness and type II error properties of the *t* test to departures from population normality. *Psychological Bulletin, 111,* 352–360.

Schaefer, C., Coyne, J. C., & Lazarus, R. S. (1981). The health-related functions of social support. *Journal of Behavioral Medicine, 4,* 381–406.

Schoenbach, V. J., Kaplan, B. H., Fredman, L., & Kleinbaum, D. G. (1986). Social ties and mortality in Evans County, Georgia. *American Journal of Epidemiology, 123,* 577–591.

Scott, J. (1991). *Social network analysis: A handbook*. Newbury Park, CA: Sage.

Seeman, T. E., & Berkman, L. F. (1988). Structural characteristics of social networks and their relationship with social support in the elderly: Who provides support. *Social Science and Medicine, 26,* 737–749.

Sharf, B. (1997). Communicating breast cancer on-line: Support and empowerment on the Internet. *Women & Health, 26,* 65–84.

Short, J., Williams, E., & Christie, B. (1976). *The social psychology of telecommunications*. New York: Wiley.

Silver, R., Wortman, C., & Crofton, C. (1985). The role of coping in support provision: The self-presentational dilemma of victims of life crises. In I. G. Sarason & B. R. Sarason (Eds.), *Social support: Theory, research, and applications* (pp. 397–426). Boston: M. Nihjoff.

Sproull, L., & Kiesler, S. B. (1991). *Connections: New ways of working in the networked organization*. Cambridge: MIT Press.

Sproull, L., & Kiesler, S. B. (1996). Increasing personal connections. In R. Kling (Ed.), *Computerization and controversy: Value conflicts and social choices* (pp. 544–475). San Diego, CA: Academic Press.

Stokes, J. P., & Wilson, D. G. (1984). The inventory of socially supportive behaviors: Dimensionality, prediction, and gender differences. *American Journal of Community Psychology, 12,* 53–69.

Stoll, C. (1995). *Silicon snake oil: Second thoughts on the information highway*. New York: Doubleday.

Suitor, J. J., Pillemer, K., & Keeton, S. (1995). When experience counts: The effects of experiential and structural similarity on patterns of support and interpersonal stress. *Social Forces, 73,* 1573–1588.

Thoits, P. (1982). Conceptual, methodological, and theoretical problems in studying social support as a buffer against life stress. *Journal of Health and Social Behavior, 23,* 145–159.

Thoits, P. (1995). Stress, coping, and social support processes: Where are we? What next? *Journal of Health and Social Behavior, 35,* 53–79.

Tichon, J., & Shapiro, M. (2003). With a little help from my friends: Children, the Internet and social support. *Journal of Technology in Human Services, 21,* 73–92.

VanLear, C. A., Sheehan, M., Withers, L., & Walker, R. (2005). AA online: The enactment of supportive computer mediated communication. *Western Journal of Communication, 69,* 5–26.

Walker, M., Wasserman, S., & Wellman, B. (1994). Statistical models for social support networks. In S. Wasserman & J. Galaskiewicz (Eds.), *Advances in social network analysis: Research in the social and behavioral sciences* (pp. 53–78). Thousand Oaks, CA: Sage.

Wallace, J. (2005). Job stress, depression and work-to-family conflict: A test of the strain and buffer hypotheses. *Industrial Relations, 60,* 510–537.

Walther, J., Anderson, J., & Park, D. (1994). Interpersonal effects in computer-mediated interaction: A meta-analysis of social and antisocial communication. *Communication Research, 21,* 460–487.

Wasserman, S., & Faust, K. (1994). *Social network analysis: Methods and applications.* New York: Cambridge University Press.

Wasserman, S., & Galaskiewicz, J. (Eds.). (1994). *Advances in social network analysis: Research in the social and behavioral sciences.* Thousand Oaks, CA: Sage.

Weinberg, N., Schmale, J., Uken, J., & Wessel, K. (1995). Computer-mediated support groups. *Social Work With Groups, 17,* 43–54.

Weinberg, N., Schmale, J., Uken, J., & Wessel, K. (1996). Online help: Cancer patients participate in a computer-mediated support group. *Health and Social Work, 21,* 24–29.

Weinberg, N., Uken, J., Schmale, J., & Adamek, M. (1995). Therapeutic factors: Their presence in a computer-mediated support group. *Social Work With Groups, 18,* 57–69.

Weiss, R. S. (1974). The provisions of social relationships. In Z. Rubin (Ed.), *Doing unto others: Joining, molding, conforming, helping, loving* (pp. 17–26). Englewood Cliffs, NJ: Prentice-Hall.

Wellman, B. (1981). Applying network analysis to the study of support. In B. H. Gottlieb (Ed.), *Social networks and social support* (pp. 171–199). Beverly Hills, CA: Sage.

Wellman, B. (1992). Which types of ties and networks provide what kinds of social support? *Advances in Group Processes, 9,* 207–235.

Wellman, B. (1997). An electronic group is virtually a social network. In S. B. Kiesler (Ed.), *Culture of the Internet* (pp. 179–205). Mahwah, NJ: Lawrence Erlbaum.

Wellman, B., & Frank, K. (2001). Network capital in a multilevel world: Getting support from personal communities. In N. Lin, R. Burt, & K. Cook (Eds.), *Social capital: Theory and research.* Chicago: Aldine De Gruytere.

Wellman, B., & Gulia, M. (1999). The network basis of social support: A network is more than the sum of its ties. In B. Wellman (Ed.), *Networks in the global village: Life in contemporary communities* (pp. 83–118). Boulder, CO: Westview Press.

Wellman, B., & Hampton, K. (1999). Living networked on and offline. *Contemporary Sociology, 28,* 648–654.

Wellman, B., Salaff, J., Dimitrova, D., Garton, L., Gulia, M., & Haythornthwaite, C. (1996). Computer Networks as Social Networks: Collaborative Work, Telework, and Virtual Community. *Annual Review of Sociology,* 22, 213–238.

Wellman, B., & Wortley, S. (1990). Different strokes from different folks: Community ties and social support. *American Journal of Sociology, 96,* 558–588.

White, H., Boorman, S., & Breiger, R. (1976). Social structure from multiple networks. I. Blockmodels of roles and positions. *American Journal of Sociology, 81,* 730–779.

White, L., & Cant, B. (2003). Social networks, social support, health and HIV-positive gay men. *Health and Social Care in the Community, 11,* 329–334.

White, M., & Dorman, S. (2001). Receiving social support online: Implications for health education. *Health Education Research, 16,* 693–707.

Wills, T. (1985). Supportive functions of interpersonal relationships. In S. Cohen & S. L. Syme (Eds.), *Social support and health* (pp. 61–82). Orlando, FL: Academic Press.

Winzelberg, A. (1997). The analysis of an electronic support group for individuals with eating disorders. *Computers in Human Behavior, 13,* 393–407.

Wong, S., Yoo, G., & Stewart, A. (2005). Examining the types of social support and the actual sources of support in older Chinese and Korean immigrants. *International Journal of Aging and Human Development, 61,* 105–121.

Wortman, C., & Conway, T. (1985). The role of social in adaptation and recovery from physical illness. In S. Cohen & S. L. Syme (Eds.), *Social support and health* (pp. 281–302). Orlando, FL: Academic Press.

Wright, K. (2000). Perceptions of on-line support providers: An examination of perceived homophily, source credibility, communication and social support within on-line support groups. *Communication Quarterly, 48,* 44–58.

INDEX

Made in the USA
Monee, IL
12 November 2026

1a842e3b-47e9-4f87-9e7f-f2438678609dR01